COLLEGE OF LIFE

and

SOCIAL SUCCESS

101 Life Stories
with
101 Life Lessons

How To Act Better, Feel Better, and Be Better

JOE GALLAGHER

1

Copyright

FORWARD

It has been said that "success" can be judged in many ways. The size of your house, the amount of money in your bank account, or the power you can accumulate. One measure of success is how you interact with the people you meet, how you treat them, how you listen to them, and how you help them.

Joe Gallagher, Joe Gal to those who know him well, is a good friend to many people, and a great friend to even more. He has fostered these friendships through social interactions as a corporate business leader, entrepreneur, life mentor, professional artist, and personal coach. The life lessons on achieving social success are accumulated in 101 stories which exemplify who Joe Gal is and how you can equally be a "success" through social interactions and thoughtful actions.

Tom Dugan-CEO Technology Services

COLLEGE of LIFE and SOCIAL SUCCESS

TABLE OF CONTENTS

COLLEGE of LIFE and SOCIAL SUCCESS

Introduction

As I entered college, I was very shy, insecure, and uncomfortable around crowds of people who I didn't know. It was a very difficult first few months for me, yet I saw others who made life look easy. Some were always happy. Some were confident. Some were interesting. Some always looked good. I didn't seem to have any of these attributes, and I hit an emotional low point as I struggled to fit in. It was during this low point that I decided to take action and change for the better.

I studied the people who seemed to make life look easy. Each had a different strength. I decided that I'd try to make each of their strengths my strengths. If I could build enough of these strengths, I could grow closer to becoming the person I wanted to be. I wanted to be a Renaissance man. I wasn't particularly smart or talented, but I believed I could build a better me if I knew how others succeeded. What I observed was that people weren't born confident, interesting, or happy. It was largely their actions which led to them being confident, interesting, and happy. I thought if I acted in similar ways, I could build endless strengths.

This book is 101 short stories about the actions I learned from others, how I turned them into habits, and how they led to my being closer to the person I want to be. They are actions that you can put into practice to help you walk easier through life with more confidence and happiness. They won't change the entire world, but they just might change your world.

COLLEGE of LIFE and SOCIAL SUCCESS

1) The Greatest Love of All

"The Greatest Love of All," sung by Whitney Houston, is a fantastic song about looking inward and learning to love yourself, which allows you to genuinely love others.

I was in my 20s and woke up with an empty feeling and no idea what my day would be like or my short and long-term future. I approached the day with overall fear and insecurity. I met some friends who I thought had it all together and I felt I was being left behind. I was hoping something good would happen to me, but I wasn't sure what I wanted it to be. I had happy moments, but I wasn't happy. My life was controlling me, I wasn't controlling my life. I wasn't who I wanted to be.

I saw people who seemed to coast happily and confidently through each day with purpose. This is what I wanted and more. I decided to make a list:

I want to be a happy person.

Have energy.

Be knowledgeable.

I want to be worldly.

Be a good friend.

Be interesting.

Have confidence.

Be generous.

Be a Renaissance man.

I studied people I knew who had one or more of these traits and I tried to figure out what actions they took that led to them. I worked each day to act like those who acted the way I wanted to. This book is a series of stories and lessons about how I lived and learned to be closer to the person I wanted to be.

Lesson: Decide who you want to be and take action to become that person. You can be who you want to be as you have control over your actions. You simply need to know what those actions should be and commit to doing them. These stories may be able to help you along the way.

2)To Be Interesting, Be Interested

To be interesting, be interested. I learned this by watching a friend from high school. Everyone was interested in being around him because he was always interested in what was going on in others' lives. When I figured this out, I began taking an uncommon interest in others until it became natural, genuine, and sincere. My relationships are far more rewarding, and I became more interesting.

My wife and I were at the Palm restaurant in Philly to meet my sister and several very interesting people in the entertainment world. We were with someone who worked with a former U.S. president as well as many top entertainers in the music and movie industries. Another was a very successful writer with many fascinating projects under his belt, including one of my favorite movies. A third was a movie producer and the fourth was a video producer. This would have been an intimidating situation for me without having learned to be interested. All had lives far more interesting than mine, yet they were circled around me on this night. It wasn't because I was telling great tales of my life. It was because I was genuinely interested in them. More importantly, my interest in learning more about them was visibly sincere.

As we sat down, I began asking questions about how this group got together, what were some of their favorite projects, and why this project in Philly was important to them. They did most of the talking with my interjecting a few questions. It was fascinating to me, and they could tell. I was interesting to some very special people because I was sincerely interested in them.

On the drive home, my wife said, "You had quite an audience." I replied, "I didn't have the audience. I was the audience."

Lesson: Show a genuine and excited interest in others and they will show a genuine and excited interest in you. Don't worry if you don't view your life as interesting. Be excited about others and you will be interesting.

3)Make It About Them

Even when it's about you, make it about them. I learned this from a roommate while attending college. When we were out with a large group celebrating something he had done, I noticed he was telling short stories about each of us and how we helped him with the achievement. He was very specific, so it was clearly sincere. Interestingly, as he gave us the credit for his success, we felt even more impressed by him.

I used this when a casual birthday party was planned for me in Marlton, NJ at a place called Champs. It was a sports bar and approximately 100 were attending. Instead of letting others honor me, I decided to honor them. I put together a slide show of 100 pictures, one of each guest with me at some other event in the past. I also brought a printed copy of each photo and wrote a personal note on the back of every one of them. I made it a point to personally hand out each photo and tell the person why they were important to me. This made certain that I spent time with each guest and made their night more than typical. This occurred years ago, and some friends still talk about it. I stopped by one friend's house recently and he had the photo on display among other family photos. The night was very special for me because I was able to make it special for those most important to me.

Lesson: Find ways to honor those who honor you and you will feel honored. Superbowl champs always thank their fans because fans are the only reason players get to play the game for a living.

4)Make It Special by Making It Personal

I have friends who live in a small town in the middle of nowhere, and yet always have large groups of friends who travel each year to attend their parties. There are many reasons for this, but one is surely that they personally contact each guest shortly after the initial general invitation is sent. They let each of us know how important we are to them and that they hope we can make it. I always feel special when they call to personally urge me to attend, so I attend.

I used this approach for an event I was planning. One of my ventures is that I am a professional artist. My website is www.JOEGAL.com in case you are curious. I was planning a private art show in Philly at City Tavern. I was hoping for good attendance from a list of 300 guests. I sent a general email invitation to the group and received a minor initial response. I thought of my friends and how they make me feel when they personally contact me after the initial invite is sent for their party. I decided to follow up with all 300 with a personal email to let each person know why it was important to me that they attend and be a part of the event. It took a lot of time, but it was worth it. More than 300 showed up, the show was 3 hours, all paintings were sold out in 20 minutes, and everyone had such a great time that I was urged to hold a show yearly.

Lesson: If you want to get people's attention, don't focus on yourself. Focus on others and they will take notice. They will feel honored, and you will get their attention.

5)Don't Be a Spectator to Someone Else's Dream

It's important to support your friends, loved ones, and family as they chase their dreams. However, if you give up on your dreams along the way, you will regret it, and others may give up on you. I learned this from an experience that my daughter went through after high school.

My daughter had dreams of moving to California, surfing, graduating from a California college, and working in the surfing business or some other business using communications skills. She was passionate about her dreams and others were excited and supportive. Because of her dreams, she met others with similar ones, including a pro skateboarder. They started dating as his pro career began to take off. The relationship became serious, and they decided to drive to California to follow their dreams. He was living his dream as sponsorships rolled in. He traveled the world for tournaments and was making good money.

As his dream grew, my daughter was supportive. She moved in with him in the sponsor team house with other pros. They had his money, so she didn't see the need to work. She relaxed on the porch as he trained, competed, traveled, and managed his career. She was having fun hanging out with the pros, so she didn't have time to surf or go to college, but she didn't feel she needed to. She told me that she was living the dream life.

Over time, the skater's dream grew, and they grew apart. He ended the relationship and moved on. My daughter was heartbroken, jobless, and homeless. She moved back home and was depressed for weeks. I tried a lot of things to make her feel better and nothing worked. I came home early from work to take her out for lunch and try to cheer her up. She couldn't get herself out of bed. She told me she was living her dream and now it was over. I asked her, "Who's dream were you living? He's certainly living his dream, but I can't say the same for you. You gave up on your dream and started living in his as a spectator. You're 18 so get back to living your dream life, not someone else's." This hit home with her, she snapped out of her mood, and told me that was exactly what she needed to hear.

Today, she is back in California living her dream while working in the surfing business, surfing every day, attending college, and surrounded by supportive friends.

Lesson: To give your best to someone else, you must be your best for yourself as well. Giving yourself to someone else doesn't mean giving up on yourself. Your dream doesn't have to be the biggest dream. It just needs to be your dream.

6)Don't Root Against Your Friends

There are plenty of people to root against in the world. Don't root against your friends. I learned this from another high school friend. He showed up to my sporting events, art shows, and genuinely rooted for me to succeed. After college he continued to get excited about my career and other aspects of my life. Not everyone was so excited. There were people who called me a friend but were quietly hoping I'd stumble. I don't know why. It could have been jealousy or simply that someone else's failure would make them feel more superior. You can guess who I'm still friends with to this day.

I remember a situation years ago when a friend of mine was starting up a new business. It was his first and, like everyone starting a new life, he needed help. We were attending an annual golf outing I held each year with 30 friends. Some of us were very excited about our friend's new venture and offered ways which we could help. Most were happy for him but didn't offer much more as they either didn't know how to help or weren't able to help. There was one friend who was in the best position to help. He was successful and had contacts which would have been very useful. He told our mutual friend that he wouldn't be able to help him. After golf, we were hanging out at Fager's Island having a beer and I asked him why he wasn't willing to help. His answer surprised me. He said, "Why would I want to help a friend who could someday be more successful than me?" I appreciated his honesty.

However, I noticed over the years that the crew quietly fazed him out of their lives, and he no longer attends the outings.

The friends who helped are very close to this day. We root for each other, help each other, and genuinely want the best for each other. When one of us succeeds, the others benefit as we all share with each other.

Lesson: If you show genuine joy in the success of your friends, they will genuinely root for you. You'll be better friends and have a greater chance for success as you won't have to do it alone.

7) If You Can, Tip Big

While attending college, a friend of mine was a part-time bartender. He depended on tips and didn't make a lot of money. Even so, I noticed that he always tipped big and early when we went out together. I was amazed at how excited people were when he tipped a little more than they expected. I was also amazed at how happy he was to do it and how much more the servers and bartenders paid attention to him for it. It didn't cost him much more, but he gained much more.

I have a few restaurants that I go to regularly. I use my friend's approach and tip big, early, and often. It is important to note that tipping big doesn't mean laying down $100 for a $50 tab. It is simply giving a little more than expected. Most of the time it is giving an extra dollar or two for a drink and a few percent over 20% for a tab. This minor amount over what is expected is always accepted with smiles, they remember me, and they give me over-the-top service. The service staff are hardworking people who live off tips and can help you have a great experience. Treat them with respect, tip big, and you will be repaid many times in return. It's not a big investment but it has a big payoff in both service and the satisfaction you get by helping others.

15, 18, 20, or more? Who, how, and when to tip? Books and articles have been written about it. There are pocket calculators and apps to help. Don't get confused by all the fuss. We are in a time when it seems everyone is asking for a tip. I've heard the term *tipping fatigue* used to refer to the stress and pain people go through when deciding when and how much to tip. I see wealthy people painfully calculating the tip, so they won't pay one cent over 20%. On a $100 tab, it's only an extra 5 bucks to go from 20% to 25%. Not very meaningful to me, but very meaningful to the servers. Rid yourself of the stress and go into the day looking to tip big, early, and often. You'll feel better and be treated better.

Lesson: Don't get caught up in the process and stress yourself with worry that you are overtipping. If a couple of dollars doesn't mean much to you, tip big. It means a lot to the people who can make or break your night with service and appreciation.

8)Let's Get Together

Don't say, "Let's get together," unless you mean it. If you mean it, do something about it. I called a business contact and at the end of the call I said, "Let's get together." He replied, "Look at your schedule and pick a date." I thought this was great. So many times, I would say it or hear it, and nothing happened afterwards to get together.

A friend and I used to hang out a lot and did some business together. We had great times but, when the business slowed, we stopped getting together. He called one day, we had a great chat, and we said we'd get together someday. A year passed, I called him, we had a great chat, and said we should get together someday. This went on for years until we stopped the madness. I said, "Before we get off the phone, we are going to put a date on our schedules to get together." We got together shortly afterwards and had a great time. We told each other we should get together again soon. Having learned from the past, we both pulled out our schedules and put another date on the calendar. We have done this after every get together. It ensures we will follow through, gives us something to look forward to, and has helped us build a very close relationship.

Lesson: Don't say, "Let's get together," unless you mean it and, if you mean it, put something on the schedule and follow through. You'll be surprised by how much more you do and the better you feel.

9)Your Past Lives in You

I was asked to speak to the football team at the high school where I used to play. Below is a portion of the talk:

"I'm not here because I'm living in my past. I'm here because my past is living in me. How you practice and play here and now will shape who you will become. If you dog it here, chances are you will dog it in life. I know this because I've seen it play out repeatedly. One of our teammates was born with great talent. However, he didn't want to put in the work at practice. He wanted nothing but big plays on the field instead of making progress step by step. He didn't hustle and his life never became all he wanted. Another teammate worked as hard as any of us but had very little talent and rarely played in a game. He was put in the game on defense towards the end of the season. He got knocked down, got back up, and trailed the runner. The ball popped out of the runner's hands, and he was there to recover the fumble. It was a key play in the game, and he made it due to hustle. He hustled in life and went on to have a good career and family life. Put in the work now, and you'll put in the work later in life as well. Give it everything you got tonight, and you will be a winner, regardless of the score."

Lessons: The decisions you make now, affect who you are now, and will also shape who you are years from now. You cannot change the decisions from the past, but you can make the next right decision today.

Start now by choosing to work hard and live with honor.

10)Be Here Now

Tiger Woods was teeing off during the 2022 PGA Championship. He was surrounded by hundreds of fans, all with their camera phones out to video his swing. Everyone was videoing except one guy who was totally focused on Tiger Woods. He had no cell phone, was holding a can of Michelob Ultra, and soaking in everything about the moment. In our world full of distractions and multitasking, this man stuck out in the crowd simply because he had the ability to be totally present. The media published a photo of him during the moment. The folks at Michelob Ultra were so impressed that they named him *Mich Ultra Guy*, gave him a supply of beer, and built an advertising campaign around him. Sadly, people like *Mich Ultra Guy* are rare.

I was out with a group trying to tell a story. Half the group was texting, one was answering his phone, several were watching the game on TV, and the others were looking around the room for something better. There was one person who was hanging on every word. He moved with me, like a dance. He laughed and asked questions to learn more and show interest. He was focused on being in the moment. He was a true pleasure simply for his ability to block out distractions and *Be Here Now*.

Lesson: Don't miss life's special moments because you are too busy videoing them. Don't miss life's everyday moments because you let yourself be distracted. *Be here now* and you will be a rare joy.

11)Play to Win, But Root for Your Friends

I've been playing golf for years with a friend who is far better than me. And while I've never actually won against him, I always feel like I have. He is genuinely excited when I hit a good shot. He talks more about how I'm playing than how he is playing. After each round, he recalls my best shots and adds encouraging words. He plays his best and roots for me at the same time. I have more fun losing against him than I do winning against most others.

I adopted this game strategy and I have much more fun and so do my playing partners. Unless you are playing for big money, the objective should be for everyone to have a great time together. It holds true for any game if you genuinely want others to do their best as you give it your best.

Lesson: Unless you are a professional or playing for big money, play to win, play for fun, but most importantly, play as you root for your friends to play well too. Root for your friends and you'll have more of them.

12)You Get One Chance to Make a First Impression

Research shows that most people make a judgement of others in less than 7 seconds. That doesn't allow much time to make a good first impression. Yet, most of us don't put much thought or effort into the first few moments when we meet or get together with others.

I have a friend who understands this and always puts special effort into the first few moments. I've introduced him to new people, and he always acts excited, shakes their hand, asks an initial question about how we know each other, and lightens up the mood. People I introduce him to always tell me afterwards how nice he seems. When he is meeting people who he already knows, he is prepared with comments and questions that make the encounter fun and interesting. These good first impressions have served him very well and has taught me not to take the first few moments lightly.

I recall when my sister was in Philly with her husband. She works in the film business as a make-up artist for shows like *Gotham* and *The Blacklist*. Her husband has his own videography company. They were at dinner with some key entertainment executives working on a film and wanted my wife and I to stop by. The restaurant was very busy. I spotted their table in the middle of the room. I remembered what I learned from my friend about the first few moments, so I took a few seconds to gather myself and think about it. I decided to make it a quick visit. I'd say my hellos, make introductions, say a few words about my close relationship with my sister, ask a question of each, and exit so we would not intrude on their dinner. This quick pause to set the stage is something I learned from my friend and found to be extremely effective in personal and business situations. It gives me confidence and makes certain I don't miss an opportunity to make a good first impression. As we walked towards their table, I stood tall with confidence and a smile, and gave my sister a big hug. I shook my brother-in-law's hand and introduced myself and my wife to each person at the table, one by one. I made sure I spent a minute or two focusing on each guest individually and asked each a brief question about their day in Philly. After a few minutes, I told them it was great meeting them, thanked them for taking care of my sister, and let them know we were going to be on our way so we wouldn't interrupt their dinner. Ten minutes after we left, my sister called to ask if we'd meet the group for drinks after dinner as the executives wanted to get to know us better. We were only there for several minutes but we made a good first impression because we took it seriously.

This may seem like a simple and unimportant interaction, but it is far from it. In my experience, the first few minutes are the most important. I am out to dinner often for personal and business reasons. Countless times someone stops by the table and most often the interaction is awkward. The focus is usually on one person, it feels like an intrusion, and most can't wait until the encounter ends. This happens with other types of encounters as well.

Lesson: Whether it's a dinner group, a group at a party, people gathered at an office, or countless other group situations, you should take the first few minutes seriously. Take a few seconds, gather yourself, think about how you'd like to engage, and put your best you forward. The more you do this, the less you'll have to prepare as it will become natural.

13)Be a Great Host from the Start

For years, I had friends and family to my house and many times I simply left the door open for them. They'd arrive and I'd yell to them to come in and that I'd be there shortly. I've held parties at clubs and let guests find me to say hello when they arrive. This seems fine and rather common. However, I've been on the other side of this as a guest. I certainly didn't feel welcome, and it made for low expectations of the night.

I noticed how excited my wife and I would get when certain friends of ours invited us to their place. For them to invite us to stay with them is a real treat for my wife and I yet they always make us feel like it's more of a treat for them. When we arrive, they always run to the door to greet us with smiles of excitement. If they are throwing a party, they stop what they are doing when we arrive to give us hugs and make us feel like we are the most important guests. They do this for all guests, and we all feel very special as a result. We see them as great hosts, we are immediately put into a great mood, and we usually have amazing experiences as a result.

Lesson: The way you greet your guests will set the tone, so be present and make them feel as special as they are. They will see you as special as a result.

14) Say Yes

I received a call from a business partner of mine who asked me for some life advice. He was reflecting on his life and trying to figure out how to make the most of it going forward. Without hesitation, I replied, "Say Yes." He laughed and asked me to explain. I told him that I do more than most people I know, which means I say *yes* often. Yet, as I reflect on my own life, my greatest regrets remain to be the things that I didn't do.

There is a quote by Mark Twain, "Twenty years from now you will be more disappointed by the things you didn't do than by the ones you did. So throw off the bow lines. Sail away from the safe harbor. Catch the trade winds in your sails. Explore. Dream. Discover." I think about this quote often. By not saying yes, I missed out on many amazing experiences with some amazing people. I also missed out on some major business opportunities. If I had said yes to every business opportunity, the successful ones would have enormously surpassed the failures and I might be writing a different story right now.

As for my business partner, he sold the business. He is currently pursuing his dream by trying to make it as a professional golfer on the PGA Senior Tour after having won the NJ, DE, and PA Amateur tournaments in the same year.

Lesson: Say Yes. Think first how you can do something rather than why you shouldn't.

15)Stop Thinking About What Could Go Wrong

If you go into something thinking about what could go wrong, you are setting yourself up for failure. Put yourself in a confident mindset by having a vision of success. My high school baseball coach taught me this.

I was in Baltimore for the annual leadership conference held by the company I worked for and was volunteered to be the key speaker for one of our sessions. There were approximately 300 of my co-workers in attendance. I wasn't much of a public speaker at the time. They asked me to give a late-night talk show style monologue which would be funny, entertaining, and tie in the corporate culture lessons we were working on at the conference. I was young, inexperienced, and so nervous that my stomach ached.

I was prepared but moments before I was set to go on stage, I was thinking about all the things that could go wrong. I might forget the words. My jokes would not be funny. I'll freeze in front of my peers. My message will not do what I was asked to do. I felt awful and was setting myself up for a disastrous failure.

Suddenly, I remembered what my baseball coach taught me. I started to think about how I felt back in my baseball playing days. I always wanted to be at bat in the big moment. I practiced hard and hoped for the opportunity to get to bat in the big moments. I dreamed about hitting a grand slam to win the game. When I was about to go to bat, I had a vision of myself hitting the homerun. It never entered my mind that I'd strike out. I didn't hit the homerun every time, but it usually went well and much better than if I expected a strike out.

I had a few minutes before the speech. I told myself that this opportunity is what I trained for, and I was ready. It's what I hoped I'd be able to do when I entered the business world and took this job. How lucky for me that I was given this opportunity. I thought about success. They would laugh and I would knock this speech out of the park.

My thoughts went from failure to success, and I felt confidence rather than fear. I walked confidently onto the stage and hit a home run. I was asked to be a speaker for several years following that performance. Before each one, I found a quiet spot to reflect on my past successes and envision myself doing a great job with what I was about to do.

Lesson: If you have a vision of success, you will likely achieve more than if you have a vision of failure. Try to recall a past moment of success to put yourself in a confident state of mind. Mine is a baseball moment that I still use today. Then, try to see yourself succeeding in the task ahead. This technique helped me enjoy the big moments rather than fear them.

16)It's Not Whether You Win or Lose. Wait, what?

There's a saying, "It's not whether you win or lose, it's how you play the game." If you go into a situation with the mindset that you don't need to win, you probably won't.

I was giving a pre-game talk to a high school football team. I asked the team if they heard the saying and they all shook their heads in agreement. We were standing on the 50-yard line. I pointed to the press box which displayed the name of the winningest coach in school history. I said, "I never heard coach tell me that it wasn't important to win. He told me to play with character, to play by the rules, and play with respect for your team, for your opponent, and for the game. But he also taught me to play to win." I went on to say, "You should be playing to win in sports and in life. You should be playing to win as a son, a friend, a teammate, a co-worker, a student, and more. And tonight, you play to win or get out of the way and let someone through that is. Success won't be given to you tonight or in life. You must earn it, so go and earn it."

Lesson: Playing with honor and integrity doesn't mean letting the other team win. Play to win.

17)Count Your Strokes

Whether it's in golf or in life, play as if someone is watching, even when no one is. But just so you know, someone is always watching.

A friend of mine started playing golf with a group of us after college. We always played for a few dollars to make it interesting. He was seen taking liberties with his score. It happened more than once but no one said anything to him. When he wasn't around, some of the boys would joke about how much better we'd need to play to beat him because of his creative scoring. That was many years ago and he has grown to be an exceptional person and a very good golfer. He keeps an accurate score now, in golf and in life. However, every now and then, I hear comments from the old gang about the days when he'd miraculously find a ball that was clearly long lost.

Lesson: Whether it's golf or anything else, play fair. Winning fair is the only way to truly win. And remember, even when you think they are not watching, they are.

18)It Could Be Worse... Seriously?

When someone has a problem and comes to you looking for help or simply someone to talk with, don't discount their issue based upon how difficult you judge the problem to be. I learned this lesson from my daughter.

My daughter was being bullied and was very sad. I tried to make her feel better by telling her about some kids with very difficult problems. I said, "It could be worse. There are kids growing up with poverty, drugs, crime, and violence." Before I had a chance to continue with the story, she stopped me. She said, "Dad, I really do feel for all the kids going through those types of problems and worse. But those are their problems. This is my life, these are the problems I'm facing, they are hard for me, and I'm having trouble."

She taught me a very good lesson that day. I try not to judge another's problem when they come to me for help.

Lesson: When someone comes to you with their problem, it's because they trust you enough to be vulnerable. Listen, be compassionate, and take the matter seriously. Help if you can and don't try to discount the issue by saying it could be worse. Problems are personal.

19)Self-Made… Not Likely

There is no such thing as self-made. I learned that from two of the most successful people I know who I once referred to as self-made. Both corrected me and explained how they would not have been able to achieve anything without the help of others. They both went on to rattle off a list of people who helped them on their journey. I was amazed that they were so quick to attribute their success to others and knew specifically who they were. They also told me they regularly let those people know how important they have been.

Shortly after the experience with my friends, I did some reflection on who made an impact in my life and decided to let them know. I started with my dad, who we affectionately refer to as *The Big G*. He is a larger-than-life Irishman who loves his family, his friends, being around people, and afternoons in a pub telling tales. He doesn't care much for material things. So, on his 70th birthday, I decided to do something I learned from my friends. I skipped the usual gift sweatshirt that would soon be forgotten. I said, "*Big G*, for your birthday I am giving you the gift of time." We hopped in my car and drove to Braddock's Tavern, his favorite NJ watering hole. We drank Manhattans as I told him stories about his life and how being a part of those stories helped me in so many ways. He tells me it was his favorite birthday. It was supposed to be my gift to him, but it turned out being one of my favorite memories as well.

Lesson: There is no such thing as self-made. Think of those who impact you and make sure they know how much you appreciate them. Do so and they will appreciate you. Do it now. Do it later. Do it often.

20)You Are Responsible for Your Own Good Time

Don't go into a situation expecting others to make sure you have a good time. If you are bored, maybe it's you who is being boring. Go into situations thinking that it is you who will make it fun for others around you.

I had recently moved to Harrisburg and was invited by a new friend for a day of bar hopping with his friends who I did not know. I was hoping to make new friends. They knew each other, the town, and the bars, so I expected them to show me a good time. I'm not sure exactly what I expected but this day wasn't it. I didn't say much the entire day as I waited for the group to start making it fun for me. They were having a great time together. Why wasn't I? At the end of the day, they dropped me off, and one of them said to me, "Well Joe, you don't say much." That simple comment changed my perspective immediately. I was expecting them to make the day fun for me. It's great when that happens. However, if you go into it with that expectation, you will likely be disappointed. Instead, go into the day with the mindset that you will be the one who makes it fun for yourself and others around you.

Lesson: Don't expect others to make sure you have a good time. Help others to do so and your good time will follow.

21) Bad Luck or Bad Practice?

When bad things happen, we often attribute it to bad luck. Sometimes it's bad luck but other times we are creating the situations leading to the bad luck. That is not bad luck. That is bad practice. Change the practice and change your luck.

My daughter lived in NJ, was always running late, and usually drove in a hurry. She logged her third speeding ticket in as many years. She showed me the ticket and said, "I have such bad luck!" She moved to California, gets up early each day, gives herself plenty of time to drive the speed limit, and gets to where she needs to be on-time. She hasn't had a speeding ticket in 4 years. She improved her behavior and in doing so, improved her luck.

Lesson: If things don't seem to be going your way, take a step back and make sure it's not your actions that are causing the problem. Bad luck or bad practice?

22) There Is No Try

Star Wars character, Yoda, trains Jedi knights. One of his lessons is that you either do something or you don't.

I hold a couple of special events each year which are by invitation. I can remember everyone who showed up and everyone who didn't. I have photos to memorialize each event. There are photos of everyone who showed up and none of those who didn't. I'm sure many of the no-shows tried their best to make it and gave me the reasons they couldn't. Regardless of how good the reasons were, I can't remember any of them. All I remember is that they didn't show up. What people remember is whether you won the game or didn't, made the sale or didn't, met your goals or didn't, and made it to their party or didn't.

I know how it feels when the people I care about don't show up. I get a lot of invitations and I show up to almost all of them. If I'm important enough to be invited, I make it important for me to show up.

Lesson: We don't always succeed, and we can't always show up. And while it is important that we try, trying isn't what is remembered. Show up.

23)Sometimes, It's OK to Run

I see it almost every day, co-workers who hate their jobs and friends in harmful relationships. Some see it as a weakness to run away from problems, so they gut it out and live on in misery. There are some problems that won't improve, no matter how hard we try. Recognizing these situations and accepting them for what they are is hard. Running is even harder. It's scary and we view it as failure. Sometimes it's the best course of action and takes courage.

My daughter was bullied in high school. She is beautiful, kind, artistic, and athletic. For some reason, no matter how hard she tried to *fit in*, she couldn't seem to find a way. After she graduated, many of the same kids were much nicer to my daughter but she was never going to be comfortable in this town. She recognized it and decided to change things rather than continue to try to *fit in* with the Jersey gang. She packed her bags and moved to San Diego where she found a fun place to live. She started a job making surfboards and enrolled in college. She met some great friends, surfs every day, has a cool job, and is a few courses from earning a degree. She didn't just run away from a bad situation. She ran to an amazing life.

Lesson: When you are in a bad situation, take a step back and assess the likelihood of it getting significantly better. If you don't see a light at the end of the tunnel, it's OK to run. In fact, it's the courageous thing to do.

24)Big Fish

I like to tell stories and I try to make them as interesting as I can while keeping them accurate and real. With cell phones in everyone's hand, story tellers are fact-checked instantaneously. I have a close friend who regularly asks me, "What is the source of your information?"

I was telling tales at a business function and getting quite a few laughs. One of my colleagues was there so I told a story about a restaurant he and I went to where they served a lot of different exotic meats. I won't go into the details of the story, but it was funny and got some laughs. When done, my colleague laughed and said he didn't remember a restaurant like that and wondered if I make these stories up. I asked him if he ever saw the movie, *Big Fish*. He hadn't so I explained that it was a story about a father who told many fantastic stories. His son didn't believe the stories and it created major problems between them. The father died and the son attended the funeral. In a surprise ending, the funeral was attended by all the crazy characters from the father's stories. They were true.

I turned to my colleague and said, "The restaurant we went to was called Blue in downtown Charlotte and you had the wild boar." His eyes went wide open, and he said he'd never doubt me again.

Lesson: Great stories are based on the truth.

25)Pick a Team

If you are watching a game with friends, it's a lot more fun if everyone has a team they are rooting for. I noticed this at a Super Bowl party I attended. Our home team didn't make it to the big game but that didn't stop us from having a party. No one cared about either team. When we arrived at the party, the host greeted us and made us pick a team, throw $5 into a bucket, and wear a hat for the team we picked. I was amazed at how passionately we cheered for our teams and took jabs at those who picked the other team. This would not have happened if we weren't made to pick a team. Everyone had a great time for the entire game.

I watch a lot of games and attend a lot of parties. I make sure I pick a team, even if my favorite team isn't playing. I also place small bets with others. This gives us a reason to keep in touch throughout the game and afterwards when we settle the bets, which are usually for who buys lunch.

Lesson: Pick a team. It's more fun for everyone.

26) Think of Tipping as Gifting

When I tipped with the attitude that I was only doing it because I had to, I did not feel good about it, and the person I was tipping usually sensed my pain. Something changed for me when I noticed a friend giving a NJ gas attendant a few dollars and told him that he was buying him a cup of coffee. My friend made the attendant's morning. I asked him why he thought the attendant was someone he had to tip. He said, "I don't look at it as someone I have to tip. I look at it as a gift for someone I want to tip."

When I started thinking of tips as gifts, my attitude about tipping changed completely. I enjoy giving gifts, so I started to enjoy tipping. I always carry some small bills in case I get the chance to give a gift of a tip and make someone's day. I do this in a respectful way.

There are people who work for tips and are appreciative because that's how they earn a living. There are some folks who don't normally get tips and are very appreciative when I tip them. I met a few people, however, that seemed insulted by me thinking they were someone I needed to tip. This happened when a contractor fixed a door at my house, and I gave him a $20 tip. He pushed it back and grumbled. I sensed that he thought I felt superior, which was not the case. The next time a contractor did work for me, I gave him a $20 tip and said, "Thanks for the great job. I can't join you, but I'd like to buy you lunch." This was a big hit and how I handle most tips when I'm not sure the proper etiquette.

Lesson: I used to wonder who I *had* to tip. Now I wonder who I *can* tip. I look for ways to tip those who are helping me. My confusion and high stress level are gone as I don't care what the experts say about who to tip, how much to tip, and when to tip. I don't care if I'm wrong in their eyes. And if I'm wrong, I'm wrong on the right side. The high side. In the process, I make a lot of people happy, including myself.

27)If They Can Do It, We Can Do It

My son loves to ski. When he was in middle school, he found a video of some kids skiing in their backyard on a homemade ramp. He showed it to me, and we were both amazed as we watched the kids having a great time skiing. He said, "If they can do it, we can do."

It was early but my son went upstairs. I thought he went to bed, but he came back down later with plans he drew for a 40-foot-long backyard ski jump. He gave the plans to me and said, "If they can do it, we can do it." I had a friend in the carpenters union and mentioned it to him, half joking. He told me he had some extra wood and could build it for us. In a moment of impulse, I told him to do it.

While we were away for the weekend, my friend brought his extra lumber to the house and built us a 40-foot-long ski jump based on my son's plan. We arrived back home to an amazing site. My wife wasn't thrilled to see a giant ramp in the yard, but my son and I were very excited. My neighbor put his arm around me and said, "Normal people put pools in their backyard."

My son and his friends had some great times for the next five years. Fortunately, no one injured themselves during the time we had the ramp. I learned a good lesson from my son, and he went on to be an entrepreneur with a graphic design business, a skateboard shop owner with some friends, and still has time for a full-time job.

Lesson: See the world with open eyes and a mentality that you can do what others can do.

28)I Could Have Missed the Pain

The song, "The Dance," sung by Garth Brooks, is about having to endure some pain to live life to its fullest. If you avoid things because there is a chance of pain, you miss the best that life has to offer.

My most successful friends have similar traits, and one is that they take risks. When things go right, there is pleasure. When things go wrong, there is pain. When I ask them, they all say, "The pleasure is worth the pain."

My brother was a Clemson scholarship football and baseball player when both teams were among the best in the country. I remember a story about him being tackled by a future NFL defensive end. He was hit so hard that he vomited. His body took a beating every day. He went on to sign a professional baseball contract with the Blue Jays and his body continued to take a beating. Years have passed, he's had countless surgeries, walks with a limp, and needs a hip replacement. Ask him if the pleasure was worth the pain and he'll tell you, "You're damn right it was."

Life is full of risks. Play sports and you risk injury. Commit to a relationship and you risk having your heart broken. Take a new job and you risk failing. Avoid risk and you risk the pain of an empty life.

Lesson: If you don't take risk, you have little hope for success and true happiness.

29)I'm Not Good at This

The best man stood up at the wedding and began his toast, "I'm not good at this." The honoree stepped to the podium and said, "I'm not good at this." The teacher on parents' night opened with, "I'm not good at this." They all had their opening comments in common. They also had something else in common. They lost all of us who were listening because they told us they weren't good, and we believed them.

I hear this opening very often. I made the mistake in using it a time or two. It may be one of the worst ways to start a speech or toast. Speaking in front of a group, no matter how small, can be very intimidating. However, we all must do it at some point. People understand how difficult it is and they will usually give you a lot of slack. However, when people hear your first words telling them you are not good, you are already off to a bad start, and it's hard to recover.

Lesson: If you tell people you are not good, they will usually believe you, and it will be an uphill battle from there.

30) They Will Let You Down

Your family is not perfect. Your friends are not perfect. You are not perfect. If you spend enough time with someone, they will let you down at some point and you will do the same. If you have a zero-tolerance policy, eventually you will have zero friends.

Two friends of mine were inseparable. They grew up together, went to the same college, traveled the world skiing together, and spent a lot of time having fun and helping each other. At one point, they both worked for the same company. One of the friends got caught up in a moment and made some moves that significantly hurt the other. This was surprising for friends as close as these two, and it took some time to rebuild the friendship. However, with some work, they are back together.

I asked him how they could still be friends after this. He said, "If I stop being friends with everyone who lets me down, I'd stop being a friend." I've learned from this, and I choose to forgive when people let me down. People are humans and humans make mistakes.

Lesson: If you have a zero-tolerance policy when someone lets you down, be prepared to have zero friends. Give others the forgiveness that you hope they'll give you.

31) Take Their Calls

I was a young sales agent making cold calls to companies, trying to reach the owners or chief financial officers. Imagine the pain I went through trying to get someone to talk with me. Most of the time, I was stopped by the receptionist or the call center. When I did get through, I was usually dismissed and treated rudely. One day, I called a company and managed to get through to the owner. He took my call and asked how he could help me. As it turned out, his company wasn't a candidate for what I was selling. He could have dropped off the call once we figured this out. However, he spent some time giving me advice and provided me with a few other company names that I should call.

I told the story of this man's kindness more times than I can count while I was living in Baltimore. I crossed paths with people who knew him and his company, so I told the story. It's likely the story got back to him which I'm sure made him feel good. More important, I was spreading positive feedback that others were hearing. It surely helped his reputation and that of his company. Personal and business success often relies on brand, reputation, and your network of positive relationships. He helped himself in all these areas by taking my call, being courteous, and helping me simply because he could.

I've learned from this encounter, and I try to respond to all calls, voicemails, and emails. Many of the callers can't help me but need help. If I can help, I usually try to. I was in their position, and I always hoped I'd reach a person that was friendly on the other line. So, I try to be that person.

Lesson: Put yourself in their shoes and take the call. You'll feel good, and you never know how helping others is going to help you.

32)We Love a Rising Star

We love a rising star. However, we only love a rising star until they rise to the top. Once they make it to the top, we turn on them for some reason.

Tom Brady is a perfect sports example. He was drafted late by the New England Patriots, so no one expected much from him. He got a chance in his second season when the starting quarterback was injured. Everyone cheered for the new kid, and he did well from the beginning. He kept getting better and we cheered even more. Surprising everyone, he led the Patriots to their first Superbowl title that year and we cheered more. We cheered until we watched him win Superbowl after Superbowl, breaking record after record, and becoming arguably the greatest of all time. And then we booed. We called him a cheater. We cheered when he lost. We tried to argue why he is not the greatest of all time.

This phenomenon is not just for sports. I've seen this often with friends and co-workers. We cheer for our friends and co-workers while they are climbing the social and corporate ladders. We are happy to help them and honored to be part of their growth. But something happens to us when they succeed, outperform us, or make more money. An ugly reality creeps in. We find fault and ways to make ourselves feel superior.

I mentioned in another story, "There are plenty of people to root against in your life. Don't root against your friends." Take pleasure and pride in the success of your friends and co-workers and they will do the same with you. When friends have success, they will take you along for the ride if you are genuinely on their side.

Lesson: Don't stop supporting your friends and co-workers when they have success. Brag about them and take pride that you were with them throughout their journey.

33)Don't Be One

My high school baseball coach gave me advice and coaching every week for three years. I'm sure he taught me a lot, but I can't think of anything specific that he told me, except for one thing. On the last day of my senior year, there was no more work to be done. I was excited and nervous about stepping out into the big world. I was standing in our school's long glass hallway, watching the buses leave for the last time when Coach appeared. It was just the two of us. He put his arm around me and said, "Gallagher, there are a lot of a**holes in the world. Don't be one."

This advice stuck with me. Some people get confused about their behavior. There's a thing called AITA where people ask others, "Am I the a**hole." If you must ask, you already know the answer.

Lesson: Don't be one.

34)See Like an Artist

When I'm not telling stories, one of my passions is art. I am a professional artist, painting in oils and acrylics. My website is www.JOEGAL.com

I've given lessons to kids wanting to know how to draw and paint. When I ask them to draw a wave from a photo, they almost always draw rows of squiggly lines. Their eyes are seeing the wave, but their mind is telling them a wave is rows of squiggly lines. Their minds are processing what they have learned and experienced from their pasts, instead of what they are seeing.

My wife and I were driving at dusk and the sky was beautiful. I asked her what color the clouds were. She said they were white because that is what she had been taught to believe. I told her that I see yellow, blue, red and some purple. I asked her to forget about the clouds and look for purple. She said she saw purple, as well as yellow, blue and red.

During the same drive, I asked her what shape the clouds were. She said round because that is what she was taught clouds looked like. I asked her to look for a cloud that looked like a puppy's head. She saw it immediately.

Seeing like an artist allows me to see the natural beauty of the world rather than the altered view our mind is telling us we see. As you look at the ocean, mountains, rivers, forests, or any view that interests you, look for lines, shapes, values, and colors. If you can simplify what you are seeing in this way, you'll be amazed by what you see. Enjoy!

Lesson: See like an artist and see a whole new world.

35)Poker is Not a Game of Chance

Life and Poker are similar at times as we usually can't control the cards we are dealt. A lot of people fold when they are dealt a bad hand. A smart player knows that it is not the cards you are dealt that matters. It is how you play the cards that counts.

I used to entertain clients in Atlantic City at the casinos. I played a lot of Texas Hold'em poker. When I played the low-stakes tables, I walked away a winner almost every time. However, when I played the high-stakes tables, I rarely won. When I was at the low-stakes tables, I was playing with low skilled players who were there for fun and free drinks. They viewed poker as a game of chance where winning was based on the luck of the cards you were dealt. The players at the high-stakes tables understood that poker was a game of skill where you win by how you play the cards you are dealt, not which cards you were dealt. The best players studied the habits of the others. They watched how each player bet and their facial expressions when cards were dealt. They calculated odds and, over time, the best player usually won.

In life and business, we are not aways happy with our circumstances. Like poker, we can't always control the cards we are dealt. It's worthless to complain about our bad luck or hope somehow the cards will magically change. We must accept the cards dealt to us and use what we know to play them to the best of our ability.

Lesson: In life, like in poker, it's not always the cards you are dealt that determines your success. It's how you play them that counts.

36)I Won't Be Offended by a Last-Minute Invite

Some of the best opportunities come at the last minute. Yet I've seen people turn down great events because they were offended by a last-minute invite. They assumed they were not the first choice, which they weren't, and this was upsetting to them. I thought this way until a friend of mine told me he won't be offended by a last-minute invite.

One of my jobs involved a lot of entertaining at lavish golf courses, pro sporting events, and nice restaurants. I was hosting three clients at a golf event when a guest canceled at the last minute. One of the guests with me at the time asked if this happened often. I told him that it happened all the time. He told me that he also entertains often, and it happens a lot to him as well. He said, "If you find yourself in this situation again, give me a call no matter how late. I won't be offended by a last-minute invite."

This was great for both of us. It's hard calling people at the last minute because we worry that they will be offended in knowing they weren't the first choice. I gave him the same promise if he had a last-minute cancellation. He and I called each other countless times over the years, attended some amazing events together, and became great friends.

Lesson: Don't be offended by last-minute invites. In fact, you should be very appreciative, even if you must decline. Do this and you will be surprised at how many opportunities you'll get. Be offended and you won't have to worry about being offended next time, because there won't be one.

37)Thank God It's Monday

The phrase, "Thank God It's Friday," was depressing to me as I pondered a life where I'd work five uneventful days each week with the hope of two good ones on the weekend. I was living in Baltimore for a company I liked and a job I loved. Even so, I couldn't wait for the weekend. On Sunday's I would get a sinking feeling as the weekend came to an end and I knew it was back to the workweek.

After a few years of TGIF, I picked up a book titled *Never Eat Alone* by Keith Ferrazzi. I'm not sure if I read the book but the title changed me forever. I started scheduling business and pleasure lunches almost every day. It helped, but I still couldn't wait for Friday. There were a lot of great sites to see in Baltimore so I started scheduling fun things on weeknights, which I would normally do only on weekends. I went to places like the Baltimore Museum of Art, National Aquarium, Maryland Science Center, concerts at Merriweather Post Pavilion, Inner Harbor, Orioles, and more. I had more things to do during the week than I did on the weekend because I had more days to work with. I moved to the Philly area, and I still have more planned during the week than the weekend. So much so, that my friends use the term TGIM around me and text me on Mondays to see what fun things I have planned.

Lesson: Life is much more fulfilling when you have seven days rather than two days for the things you love to do.

38) Throw Them a Line

It's not easy being the stranger in a crowd of people who know each other.

It was a Philadelphia Eagles gameday and I arrived early to meet some friends who were having a tailgate party in Lot E. It's a big lot, I couldn't find them, and no one was answering their phones. I walked around the lot several times. It was filled with thousands of people. A guy at one of the tailgates noticed that I walked by a few times and was obviously lost and on my own. He stopped me and asked, "Can't find your tailgate?" I laughed and said, "Seems so." He invited me to hang out at his tailgate until I could reach my friends. He handed me a beer and introduced me to his buddies. He asked some questions and quickly made a connection as he is a contractor who does some home renovation work in my town. We've stayed in touch since that day. I was very appreciative of him for saving me from being alone in a crowded lot. I've mentioned him and his business to some friends to help market his work.

I know how it feels to be alone in a crowded room. If I see someone in that situation, I try to throw them a line and bring them into a conversation with my crew. I've met some very interesting and appreciative individuals.

Lesson: If you see someone who seems lost in the crowd, imagine it was you. Throw them a line.

39)Miller Time

I attended a business function for charity years ago in New York City. It was well attended by Wall Street's masters of the universe, professional athletes, business leaders, and philanthropists. In the middle of the room was what appeared to be an ordinary man in a group of A-listers. Everyone was gravitating to him. He was, *The Man*. I found this very interesting because he didn't appear to be anything special. He wasn't big, strong, famous, or with model good looks. Yet there was no question that he was, *The Man*.

I've come to know him well over many years as a friend and business associate. Every time we get together it's an adventure for all involved. I refer to our time together as *Miller Time*. More important than the good times he has given his friends, he inspires us to be better by the example he sets. I've been around him enough to understand some of what makes him special. It's surprisingly simple to say and more surprisingly difficult to do. He is selfless with an uncommon genuine interest in people who he tries to help in any way he can without asking for anything in return. He is a giver, and the universe gives back. Simple as that!

Lesson: Develop a selfless and genuine interest in others and they will do the same with you.

40) Four Touchdowns

I played football growing up and had visions of my son doing the same with me as the coach. He chose ice hockey, and my football coaching career was over before it started. He came home one afternoon and said he played football with the boys in the neighborhood. I asked him how it went. In a soft tone he said, "Good, I scored four touchdowns." He went up to his room and my heart sunk.

My son knew I was a football fan. It was the first time that I heard of him playing neighborhood football so, of course, he couldn't have scored four touchdowns. I felt terrible that he thought he had to say he scored so many touchdowns to try to make me proud of him, knowing how much I liked football. I learned a valuable lesson that day. Going forward I made it clear to him that I was proud of him for making the ice hockey team and for all other activities he chose.

Later that afternoon I learned another valuable lesson. His buddy stopped by and said, "Hi, Mister G. Sean was great today. He had four TD catches. Is he around?"

Lesson 1: Be supportive of the choices others make. They are their choices, not yours.

Lesson 2: Don't jump to conclusions.

41)Guilty as Charged

Own your mistakes and move forward.

I was dealing with an issue and confided in a friend. He slipped and the word got out. It wasn't a major issue, but he surely knew he shouldn't have talked about it. The next time we were together, I mentioned it. He didn't think it was him that let the word out. I explained the chain of events, which helped him remember, and he immediately said with excitement, "Guilty as charged!" We both laughed and still joke about the incident years later.

If you make a mistake, acknowledge, apologize, and move forward together. Otherwise, your denial will make things worse and lead to grudges and mistrust. I can't remember what the issue was, but I do remember *Guilty as charged*, and I'm still laughing together with my great friend.

Lesson: Acknowledge, apologize, and move forward together. Deny and you will go on your separate ways.

42)Bigger Better Deal

If you tell someone you are going to be there, don't cancel because you found something better to do.

A group of friends planned a golf outing, and we were all committed to it. When the date approached, one dropped out. We found out later that he was invited to an afternoon on another friend's boat and liked that opportunity better. He went for what I call *The Bigger Better Deal.*

It doesn't feel good when someone cancels at the last minute to do something they feel is better than your event. It's a poor move and one that will get you fewer invites going forward. We played without him during the outing and for future outings as well.

Lesson: There are times when we must cancel. Make it few, always with a very good reason, and never for *The Bigger Better Deal.*

43)I Had a Purpose Before You Had an Opinion

Jalen Hurts, Eagles quarterback, responding to critique by a reporter said, "I had a purpose before you had an opinion."

My brother was an outstanding high school athlete with a dream of playing professional football or baseball. It's a hard road and very few succeed. There were plenty of doubters, including the athletic director of the local college. He wanted my brother to attend the school. My brother wanted to play for a major university to give him a better chance to make it to the pros.

After turning down the local college, the athletic director told my father that his son would never play major college sports. He went further to say he'd kiss my dad's a** on the square in Lancaster if he got in for one play.

My brother wasn't offered a scholarship and some doubters spoke up. My brother wasn't deterred. He went to Massanutten Military Academy for a year to grow and build his skills. A year later, he was offered both a full football and baseball scholarship to Clemson University. He was a starter on a baseball team that was number 3 in the country. He was backup quarterback on a football team that was number 16 in the country, and he played in most games. Following his second year at Clemson, he was drafted in the 3rd round by the Toronto Blue Jays.

My brother never gave up on his dream, even though others gave up on him. The athletic director never did meet my dad on the square.

Lesson: Stay focused on your purpose and filter out the doubters.

44) Two Too Many

I was at a sports bar watching the Superbowl. It was crowded and I had been there for hours drinking my favorite bourbon. As the game was coming to an end, there were a few questionable penalty calls and I started yelling at the TV. The guy next to me asked, "How many of those bourbons have you had?" I've seen fights break out for less. Instead of getting angry, I simply answered, "Two." We both laughed. I know that if someone feels the need to ask me that question, the answer is always two. What I mean is, two too many.

I quietly put down my bourbon, ordered a glass of water, and handed the car keys to my wife.

Lesson: If you've crossed the line and someone calls you on it, don't let pride get in your way. Take a step back out of appreciation, not a step forward out of defensiveness.

45)What Do You Do?

I was at an event in Philadelphia many years ago. I didn't know most of the people in attendance. I was asked, "What do you do?" more times than I can remember. My answer was, "I'm in insurance." This led to some very boring and short conversations. This question was the most common I was asked for years and may still be number one.

We are regularly asked "What do you do?" when what people really want to know is, "Who are you?" In absence of a comfortable way to ask who someone is, we ask, "What do you do?" or worse, "Where do you work?" I work in insurance but that is not who I am. We are so much more interesting than what we do for a living. While we know the question is coming, we are rarely prepared. So, we answer insurance, carpenter, student, or whatever we do. This is not the best start to a conversation. It is very limiting as to how people will view each other.

I never felt good when this came up and I would answer that I was in insurance. I thought about it and decided to be better prepared. I want people to see who I am and give them several different ways to connect with me. My response changes as I change. For now, I might respond, "Well let's see. My wife and I live in Jersey and are empty nesters now that our kids have moved out. We saw them recently in Park City for a ski trip. I am a professional oil painter, own some franchises, but make most of my living in the insurance industry." This is far more interesting than, "I'm in insurance." More importantly, it gives the other person several ways to connect. They could be a skier and we could talk about the Park City trip. They might be curious about what type of franchises I own. They can ask about my kids or wife. They will likely ask about my oil painting business. If all that doesn't interest them, we can talk insurance or move on to the next person who will probably ask, "What do you do?"

Lesson: You will often be asked, "What do you do?" for the rest of your life. Be prepared, and you will be more interesting.

46)Don't Keep Score on Friendship

After college, one friend stuck out above the rest of us. He called many of us every week to keep us connected as we were spread all over the country. Week after week he'd call me. I felt bad at times that I wasn't calling him. I either felt I was too busy or simply didn't think about it. The rest of us would talk about how great he was as a friend for keeping us all engaged. One night he called, and I thanked him for being so good about calling. I apologized that I didn't call him as much as he called me. He said, "I'm just happy we are friends that stay in touch. I don't keep score."

It was a *wow* moment for me, and I learned from it. If it was about keeping score, he would win as a better friend. Fortunately, it is not about keeping score. I decided to be one of the guys that makes the calls. I have a lot of very good friends who I call regularly. Most of them rarely call me. It doesn't bother me a bit because I don't keep score.

Lesson: Don't sit back and wait. Be the one who reaches out unconditionally. Don't keep score.

47)This Ain't About Fishin'

"Just Fishin" is a song by Trace Adkins where he talks about creating memories with his daughter when she was a little girl. He fishes with her to spend time and build a bond between them. The daughter thinks they are just fishing.

My daughter and I fished together for years. I put together a slide show of our fishing together and played the song. Years later, when she was older, she'd come home later at night and ask me to play a couple of games of pool before going to bed. She lives in California now and was recently home for the holidays. We spent some time playing pool while she was home. During one of the games, I told her how much this time meant to me. She said, "And you thought we were just shooting pool."

Lesson: Find things you have in common and make them traditions to do together with those you love. Live, learn, and grow together.

48) A Great Life Takes Effort

You have to take the time and make the effort to have a great life. It won't happen by accident.

I was in Canada at a conference and was heading to lunch with a friend. He lives a more exciting life than anyone I know. We were an hour early for our reservation. As we walked towards the restaurant, we saw some seaplanes taking off. I thought to myself that it looked like a very cool thing to do and the people on the plane were lucky. It never occurred to me to get on one of those planes right there and then. I looked at it as if it was too much trouble with only an hour before lunch.

My friend looks for adventure. He looked at the situation as an opportunity and a great way to fill the hour with something new and exciting. He walked into the office and asked if he and I could take a quick flight to Whistler Mountain and back. They offered us two seats with the 4pm group. That wouldn't work. I would have given up, but not my friend. He said in a very friendly voice, "We were thinking about going right now so we could be back for our lunch appointment." She called a pilot over, he agreed, and the two of us were in the air a few minutes later. It was a great experience and an amazing memory.

Lesson: If you want a great life, you have to make the effort. It's worth it.

49)Some Battles Just Aren't Worth Fighting

There are battles that need to be fought and there are those to simply drop. A friend called asking me for the name of a real estate attorney and emphasized that he needed someone tough. I gave him a name. He explained that the homeowners' association billed him late fees for missing and late payments. He had copies of checks to prove he had paid but may have sent a few of them late. He got into an argument with the HOA accountant. Future checks were returned as damaged, even though they were in good condition. The back-and-forth battle eventually led to the accountant threatening to take possession of the home for his failure to pay the late fees. On principal, both my friend and the homeowners' association were about to lawyer up. I learned that the fees my friend was being told to pay totaled only $257.

I'm not sure how this simple dispute got so out of hand that both parties felt they needed an attorney. The lawsuit would take months, be quite expensive, and cause major stress for everyone involved. The homeowners' association should have waived the fees. However, even if they would not, my friend should have paid the $257 and moved on. Less stress, less money, and one less thing.

Lesson: Some battles just aren't worth fighting.

50)Help Others and You Help Yourself

One of the best ways to learn is to teach. It seems the same goes for helping yourself through helping others.

Everyone goes through rough patches. I've had my fair share. My wife was going through one and was having a tough time pulling herself through. She was very focused on herself and her troubles. During that period, she met some people at our church who needed some help with their efforts to help the homeless in Philadelphia. She immediately volunteered to help. From there, she volunteered to help other groups. She volunteered her time to help counsel individuals going through tough times. She devotes time every day to help others.

When she stopped focusing on herself and began helping others, she helped herself along the way. This has been going on for years and she has never been more at peace with herself. I've had a front row seat and her journey has helped me as well.

Lesson: Help others and you are helping yourself along the way.

51)Don't Do It for The Credit

Help people because you can, not because you want the recognition.

My father was in the hospital recovering from a stroke. I used the time in between visits to organize my parents' important papers. I found a box of newspaper articles, most of which were from my brother's sports days. Mixed with them, I found a plaque and an article showing my dad being handed the plaque by the mayor. It was an award in recognition of "Citizen of the Year" for his work helping the people of Lancaster. I never knew about it, and he never mentioned it. I was extremely proud. Proud that he earned it, but prouder that he did not care about the recognition or credit. He helped people simply because they needed it, and he was able to do so.

Lesson: Whatever your situation, there are a lot of people who can use your help. Help them because you can. That should be credit enough.

52)Lost in the Details

I often talk with people who spend a great amount of time and effort mining data so they can prove that the obvious is wrong. Some people fall for this because they can't dispute the data. Their vision is clouded by minor statistics, and they lose sight of the larger picture.

I was having dinner with a group that included a future star leader of the company I was working for at the time. He was very good with spreadsheets, like a lot of young technically inclined managers. He loved being good at collecting and managing data. Like many young managers, he liked to think that data was what he needed to give him the answers to all questions. Unfortunately, it's not that easy. I've seen two managers use the same data to support their argument for opposite points. Leadership requires decision making and while data is important, it is only one ingredient to good decision making.

As the night progressed, conversation shifted to sports. The young manager proudly chimed in and said, "I've done the research and Michael Jordan is not the best player in the NBA." Jordan was still a player at the time of the dinner. He rattled off minor statistic after statistic, made comparisons to lessor players, and spoke in detail about why Michael Jordan was, in fact, not the best active player in the NBA. After he finished his report to us, I simply said, "That's interesting, except you forgot one thing. Michael Jordan is the best active player in the NBA." Everyone else at the table agreed.

I'm not sure my friend and co-worker agreed but he has since mastered the balance necessary when using data and is a very successful leader.

You can shape data to get the answer you want. That doesn't make it the right answer. It's easy to get so wrapped up in the small details that you can't see the full picture.

Lesson: Michael Jordan was the best player in the NBA. And don't let small details blur your vision of the obvious.

53)Keep It Simple

We often find ourselves in situations where there are so many variables that we can't understand what's happening. I find it best at times to focus on the single most important issue and filter out the other issues that create confusion. By doing this, you can often figure out what is happening. My father was especially good at this.

My sister is quite fantastic, but I remember one guy who didn't get it. She was dating him over the summer. She really liked him, but he dropped off the map when he went back to college. No calls, no notes, no contact in any way. She was hurt and spent weeks trying to figure out what was happening. Many of us talked with her and tried to help figure it out. After more than a month of mystery, my father decided to step in. He met with my sister for lunch. When she sat down, my father asked, "Do you want to know why he isn't calling you?" Desperate to understand, she said, "Please, please tell me." To which my father replied, "Because he doesn't want to." End of mystery, both laughed, the guy's loss, and my sister was able to begin moving on.

Lesson: When situations get confusing, filter out all the minor issues and focus on the single most important issue to help you understand what's happening.

54) Hear What You Want

There is a growing number of haters in the world who seem to feel good about themselves by trying to tear down others. They also seem to yell louder than those who offer support and encouragement. Phase out their voices and listen to those who build you up.

There's a great TV commercial from a few years ago for Beats headphones. Kevin Garnett gets up from his chair as the TV plays ESPN with announcers criticizing KG. They bash him for recent mistakes and talk of him being too old to hang with the young players. He grabs his headphones and is seen walking to the team bus as fans yell at him and throw eggs. He sits on the bus as he listens to "The Man" sung by Aloe Blacc. He's at peace and ready for the night's game.

I kept the commercial in mind as I visited numerous art galleries to try to convince them to represent me and sell my paintings. Most gallery owners were quite rude and insulting. They didn't seem to care what my art looked like or to learn anything about me. One gallery after another led to nowhere with none of them even willing to look at my art. This surprised me because without artists, there is no need for galleries. I could have let their comments change how I felt about my art and myself. However, there were those outside the galleries who loved my art and I thought more about their comments. I never did get the big gallery contract. Instead, I developed an on-line art business and funded my own art shows. Today, I am selling more art than most of the galleries I visited because most of them failed and filed for bankruptcy.

Lesson: Don't let hateful words from other people derail you. Hear what you want, not what they want.

55)Through Their Eyes

I was in church with my family as the collection basket was being passed around for the weekly offering. I reached into my pocket and realized that I had forgotten my wallet. I asked my young son, who was sitting next to me, if he had any money. He opened his wallet and gave me everything he had which was three dollars. I dropped it in the basket and said, "That's a new low donation for me." He replied, "That's a new high for me."

I was looking at the situation solely from my own point of view. For me it was simply stuffing the basket. I didn't consider my son's point of view. For my son it was everything he had in his wallet, he gave it up willingly, and it made him feel good.

Lesson: Your view of the world expands greatly when you think about how things look from others' eyes rather than only your own.

56)What If Your Mom Was Driving That Car

Road rage is a serious problem. I'm not sure what happens to us or why it happens when we get behind the wheel of a car. Perhaps it's a false sense of anonymity. For whatever reason, nice people become mean, calm people become stressed, and patient people are running others off the road because they dare to drive as slow as the speed limit.

I'm from New Jersey where we seem to treat driving like a competition. The state did a survey and one of the multiple-choice questions was, "Why don't you use your turn signal?" The most popular choice was, "I don't want to alert the enemy."

I used to be one of the offenders and it made for very stressful, white-knuckle driving that put me and my family in danger at times. After years of this insanity, I was driving with my wife and was annoyed with the driver in front of me. My wife said, "What if your mom was driving that car?" Of course, she wasn't driving the car in front of me, but it did make me pause. I've used that thought to keep me in check. I now refer to myself as a kinder, gentler driver. I have been able to eliminate a lot of stress in my life as I'm behind the wheel for long drives every week. And I've learned that I usually arrive about the same time as I would have if I was one of the *aggressive* drivers.

Lesson: Driving doesn't have to be a dangerous and stressful competition. It's well within your control.

When you get upset with the car in front of you, think as if your mom was the driver. I've cleaned up my act and I feel so much more at ease when I hit the road.

57)Old Fashioned Traditions

Traditions give us a sense of belonging. Intentionally create them and give everyone something to look forward to and share together.

Friends of mine from college got together for a weekend of golf and fun. We shared a lot of laughs, played golf, and sat around a fire telling old tales. What I remember most from the weekend was a tradition which was started by one of our friend's family. One of the patriarchs used to make his special recipe Old Fashioned cocktails at family gatherings and it became a fun tradition that was passed on. An Old Fashioned is a cocktail made by muddling sugar with bitters, whiskey, an orange slice, and a cherry. He rolled up with his cooler full of the ingredients, told us of his family tradition, and then made each of us one of his special Old Fashioned cocktails. We toasted to great friends and now we are part of a new tradition. I'm looking forward to our next get-together and feel more connected due to this new tradition.

Lesson: Find something you can do with your family and friends and make it a tradition. It's a tie that binds people together and makes gatherings special.

58)Someday, Another Word for Never

The movie *Knight and Day* is a favorite of mine and my daughter's. We've watched it countless times together. In it, Tom Cruise's character, Roy, lists all the exciting things he'd like to do in his lifetime. Cameron Diaz's character would like to do the same things and says, "Someday." To which, Roy explains that *someday* is another word for never.

If you've put enough thought into the things you'd like to do, and I hope you have, put even more thought in how you are going to do them and make them a reality. My daughter seemed to learn well from Roy. She talked for years about her dream of living in San Diego. But it wasn't just talk. She put it down on paper and gave a lot of thought about what she needed to do to make it happen. A lot of people talk about what they want to do but few do what is needed to see their dreams through.

In July 2019, she and I were in San Diego together as she was signing her first California lease. As she held the pen on the line for the date, she asked me what day it was. I said, "It is July 12th. She said, "It's *someday* dad. *Someday.*"

Lesson: Don't let *someday* turn into *never*. If there are things you want to do, put them down on paper and start working today on what you need to do to make them happen.

59)Friends are Not Possessions

"I introduced them and now they are out to lunch without me. It's my friend and they wouldn't even know each other if not for me." I hear this type of comment often. I've seen many relationships deteriorate because of situations like this. I've seen bullying in high schools for this. We love having friends so much that we don't want to share them out of fear we won't be as important. We treat them like possessions, and we want to keep them for ourselves. This is not a very good way to be a friend. It adds a lot of tension and stress to relationships. Treat friends well and share them with others. If they develop a great relationship with someone you introduced them to, take satisfaction in knowing you made several friends' lives better.

One of my closest friends was very good at building a group of connected friends. He and I were together years ago and he told me he had a friend he wanted me to meet. He said this guy and I would be great friends as we had a lot in common. We arranged a night out. That was over 30 years ago. The three of us are still great friends to this day.

I learned from this and paid it forward. I introduced the new guy to another one of my friends who I thought would be a good person for him to get to know. This continued and we have a very large group of friends who get together often. Sometimes we get together in large groups but mostly it's in smaller groups. We never get upset when others get together without one or more of us. We can't possibly include everyone in everything we do.

Lesson: Don't treat friends like possessions. Treat friends like friends. Look at friendship with abundance and share. I can remember most of the friends who I introduced to each other, even if they don't. It makes me feel good to have helped others grow their group of friends.

60)Be Passionate about What You Do

I was working in Baltimore after college for an insurance company. During a dinner with clients, the group had spent most of the night talking sports. One of the guests said, "Let's change it up. Joe, what do you wish you were doing if you weren't in insurance?" I replied, "I'd be playing shortstop for the Baltimore Orioles." The group laughed and the person asked, "OK. If you weren't shortstop for the Baltimore Orioles, what would you be?" I replied, "I'd be playing third base for the Baltimore Orioles."

I hear parents, teachers, advisors, and others telling kids to do what they are passionate about. This sounds good but, in my case, being the shortstop for the Baltimore Orioles wasn't going to happen no matter how passionate I was about baseball. In some cases, it does happen and that's fantastic. My nephew is passionate about baseball, and he is living his dream as a major league catcher. However, this is rare. What we are passionate about is usually not what we are going to be doing to make a living. I've also noticed that for many who make their passion their job that they lose at least some of the passion over time.

I wasn't passionate about insurance when I started my first job in the industry, and I'm still not. I am, however, passionate about my job. I was grateful for the job and the opportunity. I was passionate about being a good teammate with this company, a good performer, a good learner, and a positive influence on others. These are many of the things that made me love baseball so much. I turned what I was doing into what I was passionate about.

Lesson: If you can find a way to be passionate about everything you do, you will always be doing what you are passionate about.

61)90% of Success is Just Showing Up

Woody Allen said, "90% of Success is just showing up." Most people agree with it, according to surveys. Yet, most people don't place enough importance on it.

Each year, I look forward to a large summer party held by some very close friends. They've been throwing the party for over 30 years. I was talking with some of the people who were invited and one asked, "Do you know who said they will be there?" Another in the group said, "We already know who will make the effort and who will not. We don't even need to ask." I thought about this and there is a lot of truth in it.

There are friends who show up, friends who don't, friends who say they will and don't, and friends that don't say anything at all. If you don't know which one you are, just ask your friends. If you don't like the answer, changing it is entirely in your control.

Lesson: Be the person who cares enough to show up.

62)Pop the Champagne

I know a lot of people who are saving a good bottle of champagne or wine for the perfect celebration. If the big day comes, you should celebrate. However, there is a saying "Life is a journey, not a destination." If you are saving for the destination, you only have one chance to celebrate. Celebrate the successes along the way.

I started my first job working with one of the top salesmen in the company. He taught me a lot about business but more about life. On days when we were both in the office, we went to lunch together. During our first lunch, he celebrated my new job. During our second lunch he celebrated me getting my first apartment. The next lunch we celebrated me passing my licensing exam. It seemed like we were celebrating something every time we were together, and it was exciting. To him, life was about celebrating all good things. He had his share of setbacks like everyone else, but he did not dwell on them. He simply looked for the next thing to celebrate, no matter how small it was. He was a happy man, and he made my time with him something to celebrate.

Lesson: Find things to celebrate in yourself and others and pop the champagne.

63)Fair Share

I was celebrating the holidays with approximately thirty people in a bar in Philly. We do it every year and we run a group tab. Most people are having a great time enjoying each other without a worry. However, there are a few that get anxious as the night goes on because they are worried that they might have to pay more than their *fair share*. The tab came and someone figured out what we owed. He asked each of us to throw in $40, which isn't a lot for the group. Even so, we were short, as several thought they hadn't had enough drinks and food to have to throw in $40 each. Instead of arguing, the rest of the group made up the difference.

If you attend group functions like this, I'm sure you have experienced the awkward end of the night tallying of the bill. It's usually the same people that try to add up who ate or drank what, to make sure everyone is paying their *fair share*. More importantly, they don't want to pay more than their *fair share*. It's also the same people who throw in extra to make up the difference for the shorts. The most interesting thing I've observed is that those who are *not* worried about *fair share* are also the people who are having more fun throughout the night.

Lesson: Rid yourself of *fair share worry*. Go into the night with the expectation that you may or may not have to pay a few extra bucks. You'll be surprised how much more fun you have when you are not worrying about an extra dollar or two.

64)More Than a Game

Taking someone to a game is nice. Taking someone on an adventure is priceless.

I live between Philly and NYC so there are major entertainment events happening nearby almost every night. As such, I get a lot of nice invitations. Most of the time, it's simply going to a concert or game and it's always fun. However, there are some hosts that can turn a game into an adventure by making the night about more than the game.

The Yankees were playing the Mets in the famous 2000 Subway Series. My father was a Yankees fan. I was neither. Good friends of mine are Mets season ticket holders and had tickets to game 5 at Shea Stadium. They never met my father but remembered from past conversations that he was a Yankees fan. They invited my father and I to the game which, by itself, was an amazingly generous and thoughtful thing to do. They are great hosts and wanted to make this about more than the game. They knew we were coming from a distance and didn't know our way around the stadium. One met us halfway, drove us to a lot, set up a fun tailgate party, walked with us to the game, and gave my father a Yankees shirt. We watched the Yankees win the series that night. They treated my father like a king and in doing so made this one of my favorite memories. It was not about the game. It was about how they went out of their way to treat my father, knowing how important it was to me.

Lesson: Turn simple things into an adventure and a game becomes so much more than a game.

65)Superman's Cape

People make a judgement about us in the first 7 seconds. Sometimes, we make our own judgement about ourselves in the first 7 seconds as well. If you wear what makes you feel good about the situation you are in, you will feel good. Dress for success.

I was in 8th grade at a tough school where fights broke out every day for things as little as stepping on someone's heel. I know that from experience. I was an athlete and usually left alone. My friend wasn't so lucky. One day, he walked into school wearing a new long black overcoat that made him look like Neo from the movie *The Matrix*. Not only did he look cool, but he also felt cool, and it made him more confident. He went from an awkward 8th grader to someone you weren't sure if you should mess with. He had a good middle school and high school experience, formed a band, and is still playing tunes today.

What you wear matters to you and to others. I took this lesson to work. When I started my first job, I was poor and nervous. Before I had to show up, I went with my mom on a garage sale trip and found the perfect blue business suit. It was a long time ago so I can't remember what I paid for it, but it couldn't have been more than $10. Even so, it made me feel like a million bucks and I went to work on my first day feeling much more confident.

Lesson: Dress for success. It matters to you as much as it does to others.

66)Until You Can't

Everything eventually comes to an end. Keep doing what you can, until you can't.

My shoulder hurt with every throw from 3rd base. I was easily the oldest on the team and my pain was masked by ace bandages and tape. It was, for most, a meaningless summer baseball game. For me it was my last game of organized baseball. Even in my 30s, my parents made every game they could, and they were there for this one. After the game, I saved the ball and hung up my cleats as a player. A few years later, I played my last game of organized basketball. It ended like many more things do as the years go by.

I was skiing with family and friends recently in Utah. At one point, a friend of mine and I were standing at the top of a black diamond ski trail in the trees. We looked down the mountain, back at each other, and said, "Until we can't" as we jumped in.

Lesson: Everything eventually comes to an end. It takes effort to keep the activities we love going for as long as we can. Get off the couch and into action. If you don't use it, you will lose it. See your friends, see your family, run, ski, golf, and more…until you can't.

67)Find Common Ground

Being in a room full of strangers can be intimidating. I find myself in this situation often. I have a friend and co-worker who I've known for most of my career. He is a very successful salesman and is also one of the best I've seen at working a room of strangers. By the end of the night, he knows everyone. He makes it look easy and makes an almost immediate connection. He prepares himself for the event and knows what he wants to do. He walks in standing tall and with a welcoming and disarming smile. He seeks out others to engage. He has some basic questions he always uses as openers, and he listens with genuine interest. Beyond these steps, the key to his connections is his ability to quickly find common ground.

I was attending a conference with him in San Antonio. We were about to go into the center, and he paused for a few minutes and talked with me about what he wanted to accomplish. He wanted to connect with a few people who could help him with an account or two. He put a smile on his face and walked into the center and introduced himself to some folks to our left. He asked what brought them to the conference and where they were from. With these two questions, he was able to get enough information to make a connection. He knew someone who lived by them, and they had a nice conversation about the town. There was an immediate trust built and he went on to ask about their business as a follow up to his original question. They worked in a related business, and they agreed that they would see each other at one of their booths. It was like watching an artist paint. I've learned from him over the years. One of the main things I try to do when I meet someone new, personally or in business, is to make a connection by finding common ground. With a lot of practice, I find I can do this in the first few minutes of any conversation.

Lesson: When meeting new people, you can make meaningful connections with them by finding common ground as quickly as you can.

68)Baseball is 90% Mental. The Other Half is Physical

Yogi Berra, Yankee Hall of Famer, said, "Baseball is 90% mental. The other half is physical." It's as funny as it is true. If you have a vision of success, you substantially improve your chance of success. If you have a vision of failure, you are more likely to fail.

I played for a top summer baseball team. We had pro scouts at many games. Four of our players were drafted by the pro teams, including my brother. A Yankees scout was at one of our games, looking at a teammate. Unfortunately, my teammate was nervous and struck out his first-time batting. When he was about to go to the plate for his second at-bat, he pulled my brother aside. My brother was not only a great player, he knew more about the game than anyone around. He asked my brother what he was doing wrong and told him that he just didn't feel right swinging the bat. My brother told him that he needed to tilt his left knee in slightly and that will give him a better stance and more power. He demonstrated what he meant, and the teammate did the same. He went to the plate with confidence and hit the first of two home runs. Later that night, I asked my brother how he knew that tilting the knee would help. He replied, "There was nothing wrong with his swing. He had it in his head that he was going to strike out. I just gave him something better to think about." Our teammate was eventually drafted by the Yankees and my brother opened *Gallagher School of Baseball* after his pro baseball career.

Lesson: Before you go into a challenging situation, see yourself doing what it takes to succeed. You will be more confident and have a far better chance of success than if you see yourself failing.

69)Common Sense is Not Common

Don't assume that things you feel are common are also what other people think is common to them. Common sense is not common.

I worked in an office with approximately 150 other people. The company decided that Fridays will be business casual attire days. There was no need to lay out all the details of what business casual attire meant because it was common sense. On the first Friday of the new dress code, we had jeans, khakis, leggings, sports coats, skirts, tee shirts, crop tops, sneakers, flip flops, and every other combination that you can imagine. We are a very diverse society and what seems common to one person may not seem so for another. The company had to be more specific and sent out a clarifying email. I've lost count of how many emails have been sent about the dress code since the start of the program.

Lesson: Common sense is not common.

70)Our House is Your House

If you want to impress someone with your house, show them your house. If you want to impress someone with more than your house, make them feel that your house is their house.

My wife and I were traveling to stay with some close friends for the first time. We are very close, but we don't get to see them as often as we'd like. This was our first time staying with them, so we didn't know what to expect. We walked in and after hugs and hellos, they said, "Our place is yours," and they meant it. They gave us a tour, key to the condo, a card access to the building and gym, and made us feel we could come and go as if it was ours. That level of comfort makes a visit very fun and relaxing. My wife and I learned from this and make a special effort with our guests, so they feel less like guests and more like family.

Lesson: Put less effort into trying to impress people with your home, and more into making guests feel at home. They will be impressed with your home, but more impressed with you.

71)Why Not Me?

There are a lot of occupations, and most people don't know what is available. If they see someone doing an interesting job, most never consider it possible for themselves. Sometimes great opportunities are right in front of us.

A friend of mine worked for a large corporation. He had a good job doing what he went to school for. However, he wasn't thrilled with the work and his manager wasn't the best. One of his responsibilities was working with vendors. He used one vendor often for which the company paid significant fees. The person he worked with at the vendor also owned the business, worked flexible hours, talked with people for a living, traveled, loved his work, and made very good money. Most people would not see what was right in front of them. The person he was working with had the perfect job, in his eyes. He asked himself, "Why not me?" He asked the guy how he got into the business. Not long afterwards, he quit his corporate job and opened his own firm for himself. He is very successful and very happy.

Lesson: Pay attention to what others around you are doing. If you like what you see, ask yourself, "If they can do it, why not me?"

72)I Like the Way You Negotiate

Negotiating is something we need to do in business and with some personal purchases like houses. Some people feel the need to negotiate everything possible. When negotiating, be fair. It's not always about getting the lowest price just because you can.

I walked into an art gallery in New Orleans several years ago after hurricane Katrina tore the town apart. The artist was a very colorful character known as *Captain*. I am also an artist, so we shared some stories. I asked how he made it through Katrina, and he told me he lost his gallery and eventually his home. He had to leave town and move in with friends while trying to rebuild his life and his art career. He was back in New Orleans trying to restore his business to pre-hurricane status.

I walked around the gallery, admired his art, and pointed out a framed print. I told him I liked it best of all his works. The price was listed at $700, which was very reasonable. I was the only one in the gallery and he seemed very anxious for a sale. He said, "Since you are a fellow artist, I'll sell it to you for $500." I replied, "I'll buy the print but only if you sell it to me for $700." He stepped back, initially thinking I was trying to knock the price down further. He quickly realized I was offering the original price and said, "I like the way you negotiate."

I could have paid less because he was desperate. I was in a position of strength but simply because I could knock the price down didn't make it the right thing to do. The original price was more than fair, and he clearly needed sales to keep the business going. *Captain* shipped the art to my house. When I opened the box, there was a very nice personal note, the print, various additional small prints, and a signed book. He appreciated me paying full fair price and gave me items worth more than the $200 I gave up. We both felt good as it was a win, win.

Lesson: Don't take advantage of people when negotiating, just because you can. Treat people fairly.

73) The Judge

Watch the news and you can get the impression that respect for authority is dwindling. I'm not always happy with how I'm being treated by the authorities, but I understand that without them, we have anarchy and chaos. Treat them with respect and you have a better chance of being treated that way in return.

My daughter was driving home from college when she was pulled over for speeding in a small town with a 25-mph zone. NJ has some hefty fines as the state also assesses fines annually for every violation point, as does my auto insurance company. A minor ticket can cost more than $1000 over three years. To make matters more painful, the town requires that the driver appear in night traffic court. When the time came to go to court, I decided I would join my daughter. It was winter so I put on a decent suit and overcoat. My daughter was wearing jeans and a sweatshirt. I told her she was going to be meeting with a judge and needed to dress with respect. She changed into a more professional look.

We arrived at the courthouse filled with a lot of angry people who were constantly complaining about having to be there. We weren't so happy ourselves. The only person more unhappy was the judge and I didn't blame her. People were very rude to her, arguing from the start, and dressed terribly.

The person seeing the judge before my daughter was there because he was driving in possession of marijuana before it became legal. He was wearing a sweater with images of marijuana leaves in total disrespect. It was funny but, like most of the others that night, he did not fare well when it came time to hear his fines and penalties.

The officer said, "Next case is 43861, Shannon Gallagher." I stood up to let my daughter get by me and the judge asked, "Attorney?" I replied, "Disappointed father." Everyone, including the judge, laughed as I let my daughter go by. My daughter immediately said, "I apologize, judge." It wasn't clear if she was apologizing for me or her speeding, but the judge appreciated the respect she was given. The judge spoke to my daughter with respect and explained why she should slow down. She assessed no points or fines. She only asked that she watch her speed and pay the court fees.

Lesson: We need the authorities. Treat them with respect, even when you are not happy about the situation you are in. They make decisions about your future.

74)If You Are Picking Up the Tab, Pick Up the Tab

If you are picking up the tab, make it special by picking up the entire tab. Otherwise, a split is a split, even if your split is 95%.

I was a guest of a business associate at a very nice golf club. I arrived early and my host was already there. He greeted me with open arms and treated me to lunch. He gave me a logo golf shirt that he picked up from the pro shop, along with a sleeve of golf balls. We played golf, which I'm sure was expensive. There were drinks and snacks throughout the day that he put on his tab. The course was top notch and he had caddies carrying our golf bags. At the end of the round, he was about to pay the caddies a cash tip when I stepped in and said, "You got the round, I'll get the tip." He thanked me but refused the offer and paid the caddie himself.

We played many times over the years and the story was very similar with him picking up the entire day's expenses. We became very close friends and one day I asked him why he never lets me help with the tip after he has picked up the rest of the day. He told me, "I just put a lot of effort and expense into hosting you for a special day. I want you to remember it that way. Why ruin it by letting you pick up the tip? The tip is a very small amount compared to the total cost of the day. It's not like me picking up the lunch, golf, drinks, and dinner with you picking up the tip and we call it even. I appreciate the offer, but this day is on me."

I've noticed the difference in how I felt when someone picked up the entire tab, including tip, rather than letting me contribute by picking up the tip. As a result, when I pick up the tab, I pick up the entire tab.

Lesson: There's nothing wrong with offering to pick up the tip, and I still do offer. There is nothing wrong with allowing someone to pick up the tip if they offer. However, if you want to make it special, pick up the full tab. It's not much more and it makes a difference.

75)Practice What You Preach

My son & daughter cheerfully walked to the basement to learn a quick lesson from a program I developed called *College of Life*. This day's lesson was about principles, the first of which was not being critical of others. As they sat down, I criticized them for a couple of things they had done earlier. My daughter cried and went back upstairs. My son just looked at me with a grin. Lesson over for them. Lesson learned for me.

Lesson: Practice what you preach.

76)You Were Born to Stand Out

Sometimes, when we are trying so hard to fit in, we forget to see the best in ourselves and lose sight that we were meant to stand out. Understanding the norms of society and the norms of the groups within society is important. However, don't give up on who you are while trying to fit in. Our differences are what make us interesting and unique.

My daughter tried everything she could to fit in with the cool kids in high school. She dressed like them, played the same sports, and went to the same places. None of it worked and she was trying to be someone who she wasn't meant to be. She was meant to be more. When she stopped trying to fit in, the true person started to stand out. She moved to California, surfs daily, has her own style, appeared in a music video, has a great group of friends, is an artist, works in the surfboard industry, and does all this while working towards a communications degree.

Lesson: Don't try to fit in by being the same as others. Stand out by being more.

77)Eat the Lasagna

As a guest at a cookout or dinner, know that the host made a special effort to prepare the meal. Unless you have a dietary restriction, eat the main course.

My mom is Italian and makes the world's best lasagna. She is known for it amongst my friends. She hosted many lasagna dinners for my teammates and their parents when I was playing organized sports. There was always one or two of the parents that wouldn't eat the lasagna and asked for a salad or something different. My mom was her usual understanding self, but several others were visibly disappointed and remembered who didn't eat her famous lasagna.

My son must have learned this lesson. He stopped by the house recently for dinner. He mentioned to me how full he was. He said a co-worker made her favorite dish and brought a large portion in for him after he had already eaten a big lunch. I asked him why he ate it after having a big lunch and a planned dinner with us. He said the woman was very proud of her favorite dish and was excited to give some to him. He wasn't going to let her down, so he ate it all and loved it. So did his co-worker. He smiled and sat down for dinner with us and filled his plate with large portions, because he wasn't going to let his mom down either.

When I am invited to someone's home for dinner, I know it's a special treat and always eat the main dish. It is a major part of the event experience. I'm never disappointed and neither is the host. I will be tested if someone serves liver and onions. Until then, "Bon Appetit."

Lesson: Hosts go to a lot of effort to impress you with the menu. Eat what they offer and enjoy. If you are on a diet, take a night off and run an extra mile the next day.

78)Getting Started

If you have a routine to start the day, you'll sleep easier and have a nice transition from the time you wake until you get rolling.

During the school year, my son would wake up to his alarm, shower, pack his backpack and sports gear, eat breakfast, and meet his friends out front for a ride to school. It's how he started his day, and it was so routine that he didn't need to think about it.

When school finished for the year, he'd sleep in and wake up not knowing what to do as he had no plan. He was bored and didn't know how to make the day worthwhile. Once he started his summer job, he woke up to his alarm, took a shower, packed a lunch, and drove to work.

I thought about how his days were when he had a simple morning routine compared to days when he had no idea what to do. There was a significant difference in the value of the days, so I decided to establish my own morning routine. I start each day as follows:

Review my schedule for the day (I put my schedule together the night before)

Exercise with local news on TV

Protein and fruit shake or eggs for breakfast

Shower

Personal emails

Personal bills

Head to the office

This jump starts me for every day. I don't need to think about how to get started and it gives me time to transition from sleep to work, or something more fun.

Lesson: Establish a comfortable morning routine to transition you from the time you wake up until you need to start the main events of the day.

79)It's the Thought That Counts

There is a saying about gift giving, "It's the thought that counts." It is true but it is not just about how much thought you put into the gift. It is about how much thought you put into the person who you are giving the gift to. You might think something is very cool, but have you thought about what the other person would like to receive? My youngest brother does this best, and my son was paying attention.

My wife devotes a lot of her time to a charitable organization which helps feed and clothe the homeless in Philadelphia. She does it quietly, so I wasn't sure if our kids, who are no longer living at home, knew about her work. One year our kids were home for Christmas. Our son was 27 at the time and we weren't expecting much as he was very busy with a lot of things in his young life, like most kids his age. He handed his mom a small envelope. In it was a card with a receipt for a donation he made to the charity she volunteered for. Somehow, he found out she was volunteering, figured out the name of the organization, and donated in her name. My wife started crying immediately. He put tremendous thought into what was important to his mom. It wasn't the thought about the gift that counted. It was the thought about his mom that counted.

Lesson: I like a gift card as much as anyone. However, I remember the person who gives me a gift with the thought of me in mind.

80)Help Their Family

Good friends help their friends. Great friends help their friends' families. Help a friend's parents or children and you will be a hero.

My parents are older and cannot get around easily. It was 2020 during the height of the pandemic. My folks live in Lancaster, PA and I live hours away so there was not much support I could give them due to the Covid restrictions. I was speaking with some friends who live in Lancaster, not far from my parent's home. When they asked about my folks, I joked that they were out of red wine. It's one of their few pleasures during the pandemic, and Pennsylvania liquor stores were shut down by the state. We talked about a lot of other things before getting off the phone.

A few days later, my mom and I were talking on the phone, and she told me someone rang the doorbell. When she went to the door, the person was gone and left several large bottles of red wine on the porch. I knew immediately that it was my friends. They cared enough to drive to Delaware and pick up the wine and deliver it. I did not ask them for help or even give a hint. They thought of this gesture selflessly. And it is something that I will always remember, far more than if they bought red wine for me.

Lesson: Help your friends and be a good friend. Help their families and you are a true hero.

81)Know Their Playlist

Music is powerful and some say you can tell somcone's personality by the music they listen to. I'm not sure about that, but I do know the type of music that someone likes is very important to them. If the person is important to you, get to know what music they like and it's one more way to grow your connection. You don't have to like the same music. They will appreciate that you are paying attention.

I listen to music videos while I paint on the weekends. "Watching You," sung by Rodney Atkins was one of my favorite hits when my son was younger. It's a great father-son story. I was in the studio working on a painting and listening to music when the song came on. My son was 14 with completely different taste in music from me. He heard the song playing, came downstairs into the studio, sat down with his arm around me, and simply watched the video. He paid attention to what music I liked and gave me a very special moment.

Lesson: Music is very important to most. Pay attention to their playlist and they will appreciate that you are paying attention to them.

82)Make the Moment

As we live our days, opportunities arise when we can turn an ordinary moment into a very special moment. Most people have their eyes closed to these opportunities and their days go on being ordinary. A few go through life with eyes wide open and make life an adventure.

My daughter was 12 years old when the song "Butterfly Kisses" by Bob Carlisle came on the radio. It's a great father-daughter song. She and I were hanging out in the basement at the time. She looked at me and said, "Are you thinking what I am thinking?" I smiled when she said, "We should be dancing." We danced for the first time and turned an ordinary moment into something very special. I thought about how we let special moments pass us by without notice. My daughter didn't let that happen. I learned from this and do my best to make special moments count.

Lesson: Be awake and alive. Look for ways to create special moments for you and others when the opportunities arise.

83)More Energy, More Accomplishments

I was in my thirties living in Jersey and had a very busy life. I was filling every minute with work and fun. I worked hard all day, played sports, went out with my wife and friends most nights, and had other fun interests that kept me running. I was high energy and loving life. During a basketball game, I did something to hurt my back. The next day, I couldn't move without pain. My energy was drained, and I didn't get much done for weeks. During that time, my parents retired at 58 and both suffered strokes not long afterwards. They recovered and it was a wake-up call for me.

Since there is heart disease on both sides of my family, I needed to take care of my body so it would take care of me. I wanted to get rid of my back pain which was draining me. I wanted to build up my body and heart strength so I'd have energy every day for the rest of my life. I picked up a couple of books. One was called *Body for Life,* by Bill Phillips. I learned how to eat better and exercise more efficiently. I eat well and exercise for 20 minutes in the morning. I saw immediate results without a crazy fad diet, only need 20 minutes to do a great workout, and have been following the program for over 20 years.

The other book was *7 Steps to a Pain Free Life,* by Robin McKenzie. This book taught me some very simple stretches and extensions which take me 5 minutes in the morning and before I go to bed at night.

They are designed to eliminate back and neck pain, and they do just that.

I accomplish a lot. My friends often comment on the amount of energy that I have. It does not come naturally. I work hard to keep my body and mind in good shape. These books helped me. There are a lot of programs and books. The important step that you take is not necessarily which program or book you choose. What's important is your commitment to what you learn by making it your lifestyle and not just a short-term fix.

Lesson: The more energy you have, the more you can accomplish. There are a lot of programs beyond the ones I use that can help you understand eating, exercise, and how to make them your lifestyle rather than a fad. Pick one, and fight Father Time with all you have.

84)Who Do You See in The Mirror?

I look in the mirror and see a slightly overweight balding guy working in a digital world that seems to move faster than I do. The company I work for is promoting younger employees who I mentored, and it seems I've reached my peak as I'm not being promoted along with them. I don't play basketball anymore because I banged up my right knee. I'd like to see my son more and my daughter lives 3000 miles away. I wish my wife would see things my way all the time. There is truth in this view in the mirror, but it is not the whole truth, and it is not the best truth.

I look again and I see a guy who exercises every morning and is in better shape than most who are 20 years younger. The teammates I mentored are moving up the corporate ladder which says a lot for my leadership and is a good feeling. I have a great career and still enjoy what I am doing. I was the oldest guy on the court when I decided to hang up my sneakers. It was great to have played for so long. My knees can't handle the basketball courts, but I can still ski the toughest slopes on the mountain. I must have taught my son well because he has a strong work ethic with a full-time job, a retail business he owns with friends, a side business doing graphic design, and still has time to get together with me and my wife every week. My daughter is living her dream in California, working full-time, finishing college, surfing every day, has lots of friends, and calls me every day. I am still happily married to the woman I love.

I have some friends who seem stressed a lot. I hear them describe their lives by listing only the negative things that are going on. I see the good things in their lives and their lives look much better from my perspective. I used to be the guy who saw the worst of my life and I was not happy. I started putting a lot of thought into what was good in my life, and I try to focus on those things. I see my life in a much better light, and I am happier. I look in the mirror and see the best of myself, which helps me face the day with confidence and joy.

Lesson: When you take a personal inventory, focus on what's good. When someone asks how things are going in your life, focus on what's good. The better you see yourself, the more the good will take over and grow in you.

85)Pretty, Attractive

There's only so much we can do to make ourselves prettier on the outside. I'll never be Michelangelo's *David* no matter how much I exercise. However, there is no limit on what we can do to make ourselves more attractive.

I was on a golf trip with friends in Scotland. There were 12 of us who visited countless pubs, restaurants, and golf courses. We are all outgoing yet, time after time, the people of Scotland gravitated to one guy. He isn't very tall, isn't in great shape, and has more hair on his back than he does on his head. His attraction was immediate, so it had little to do with what he had to say or who he was.

As the trip went on, I watched this happen and tried to figure out what was different about him. By the end of the trip, I came up with a simple answer. Most of us walked into places with a flat look of curiosity as we were in uncharted waters. He walked into places with a huge smile on his face and a disarming way about him that says, "I'm a good person and I'm happy to be here with you, even if I don't know you yet."

Lesson: There is a lot of truth in the saying, "A smile is worth a thousand words." Smile more.

86)Life Is Not a Race

The world is in a hurry. Go to school, go to college, get a job, get married, move up the corporate ladder, buy a house, have kids, and be a grandparent. This is known as the *Traditional Life Path*. There is often great pressure to stay on track with peers on the traditional path. Don't steer off course and don't fall behind or the critics will shout out.

There is nothing wrong with the *traditional path*. I was on the *traditional path* for most of my life, so I felt this was best for my kids. But it is important to know that it is not the only path to happiness and success. I learned this from a lot of successful people I know, including my kids.

I pushed my son to follow the path because that was what everyone else was doing and I didn't know any better. He came home one day, put his arm around me, and told me he wanted to go in a different direction but was concerned he'd be letting me down. I was devastated, not because he was letting me down, but because he thought he was by wanting to go a different route in life. It opened my eyes. I gave him my support for the path he wanted to choose, and he went his own way. He has his own retail shop with some friends, he does graphic design work on the side, and works full time at a promotional products company. There are more ways than one to happiness and success.

My daughter was under pressure by the locals for not keeping pace. She was questioned for having dreams they deemed outside her range. She was going to a local college and received some flak for not having graduated around the same time as her high school classmates. She was not keeping up with the norm. Having learned from my son's experience, I told her that life is not a race, choose a lane that works for you. She packed her bags, moved to California, works in the surf industry, surfs every day, and is close to earning a communications degree from a CA college. There are more ways than one to happiness and success.

Lesson: Life is not just a journey, it's your journey. Go at the pace that works for you and enjoy the trip. Don't be so anxious to get to the end because it is, after all, the end.

87)Jack of All Trades or Master of One

My son's 8th birthday party was coming up and I wanted to entertain the kids. Instead of hiring a juggler, I learned to juggle. My daughter's 6th birthday was soon so I learned how to make balloon animals. I wanted to learn about investments, so I took a 6-month night course. I had some art skills passed on from my mom, but I wanted to become a professional, so I took years of oil painting lessons. I wanted to learn to what makes a good public speaker, so I took a Dale Carnegie course. My friends were interested in having me officiate their wedding, so I got certified and read books on how to perform a ceremony. I wanted to improve my sales skills, so I worked with a coach. I wanted to be a leadership coach, so I took courses and got a certification. Chess, skiing, writing, and countless other skills that I observed in others and interested me, so I learned them myself. While I'll never be able to take a course to improve my 40-yard dash speed to pro level, there aren't many things we can't learn if we have the desire and put in the time and effort.

Some will advise you to do one thing, do only the one thing, and do it well. I have friends who do one thing and are successful and others who are not. Some of them are happy but most are not. There is so much we can learn and experience. Why limit yourself and limit your life? Even if you have one outstanding talent or interest, don't let that limit you from developing others and living a life of abundance.

Renaissance man: a person with many talents or areas of knowledge.

I am a fan of Leonardo da Vinci and the way he lived his life as the ultimate *Renaissance man*. He lived his life with the philosophy that one's capacity to grow is limitless. Following this has led me to learn many skills, have many interests, be more interesting, and be able to find common ground with almost anyone I meet.

Lesson: Be multi-dimensional. Life will be more interesting, and so will you.

88)Be a Chameleon

Definition: a person who changes behavior according to the situation.

I've seen many people struggle with this concept as they feel they can't be their authentic self while adjusting their behavior in differing circumstances. I see it differently. Stay true to your core beliefs but be aware of your surroundings and modify your behavior accordingly. People who are able and willing to do this are people who I've seen have greatest success in business, more joy with their families, and with the most meaningful friendships.

I arrived early to the stadium for the Giants vs Eagles NFC Championship game. I had four tailgates to go to before heading into the stadium. I stopped by the first, which was a group that runs a more sophisticated tailgate with our local wine store manager serving some expensive wines in real stem glassware. There were roughly 50 people at the party who were dressed nicely and chatting in small groups. I bounced from group to group and had some nice conversations and moved on.

The second tailgate was a major production. It was hosted by one of the most successful businessmen I know who is also one of the most politically powerful in the state. It was invitation only with security guards monitoring the tent. Some were in suits and the rest looked more prepared for a meeting than a football game. The group was serious, so I was serious.

I moved on to the third tailgate which was the typical large and crazy Eagles tailgate with a band, burgers, beers, and shots of Jack Daniels being passed around. I was loose and having a great time singing the Eagles fight song and goofing around with my rowdy friends.

The last tailgate was a smaller group of some of my best friends where I was fully relaxed with my guard down getting ready for the game. Each tailgate was very different, every event was fun, I was still me, but my behavior was different at each, yet I was always being myself.

Lesson: Being true to yourself doesn't mean behaving the same in every situation. Be aware of your surroundings and adjust like a chameleon. You'll be appreciated for who you are but also for how you can adapt to those around you.

89)I Don't Judge... Of Course, You Do

I was out with a group of friends. There was someone across the bar that was causing a commotion. One of my friends said, "Look at that jerk making a fool out of himself. But we can get a little crazy ourselves, so I don't judge." Too late, you already did.

We are being judged almost every second of the day and we are judging others. Call it evaluating. Call it constructive criticism. Call it what you like but call it judging. In the world of cancel culture, some are confusing judging with being judgmental. There is a huge difference. To judge is to form an opinion. Being judgmental means having an excessively critical point of view. In fact, we are taught to judge, and it is a fundamental part of our daily lives.

We are judged on our grades.

We are judged on job performance.

We are judged on how we look.

We are judged on how we talk.

We are judged on how we live.

We are judged on ...

You get the picture. Like it or not, judging and being judged is life. Ignore this at your peril. Instead, be aware and take control of how you judge and how you are being judged. I've heard people say they don't care what other people think. I've heard it but it's never true. In fact, those who say it are likely to care more, and use the saying as a defense mechanism.

Lesson: Don't ignore that judging and being judged is a fundamental part of life. Be careful not to step over the line to being judgmental. Control how you judge and how you are being judged.

90)Don't Be Easily Offended

With a group of friends telling tales and trying to have fun, it's easy to find offense in some things that people say. If that is what you are looking for, and you do it enough, you'll have to find new friends because no one will feel comfortable around you.

I was attending and outing with a group of close friends and some of their friends. Most of us got along, but one of the newcomers seemed to get upset during every conversation. He took everything as a personal attack, and it was uncomfortable. The group started to be careful about what was said around him. Eventually, he became the guy we tried to stay away from. He later became the guy that wasn't invited but talked about. And finally, he was the guy who was forgotten.

Lesson: Be a participant in cancel culture and eventually you will be canceled. Look for the good in people's words and actions. You will be happier and so will everyone around you.

91)Want To Remember More? Care More

The greatest leader I worked with was so strong that the company formally named "Frank-like" a value we all needed to strive to achieve. I worked with him for many years and was amazed by his memory. He remembered everything about the company's history but more important, he remembered small details about everyone's life and brought them up in conversations. I was talking about this with a co-worker, and he said, "He remembers because he genuinely cares."

Years later, my son was attending college. He didn't have the top grades in high school, and he struggled in college the first year. For his third semester, he was able to choose a list of classes that he cared about and were in the field he wanted to pursue. He was enjoying school much more and it was quite a pleasant surprise when the Dean's List certificate arrived in the mail. He was the same person he was a few semesters ago, but he was able to understand and remember the information this semester because he genuinely cared.

Lesson: If you care more, you will remember more. Care more.

92)Who's Your Favorite Team?

I know who my friends cheer for. Tom is Bama, Jeff is Raiders, Drew is Arkansas, Scott is Dolphins, Phil is Mets, and the list goes on. Knowing their team gives us common ground and gives us a great way to stay connected.

I am a Clemson fan as my broker played for them, and my friend Tom is a Bama fan. Both football teams had great runs and played against each other numerous times in recent years. Tom and I placed fun bets on each game and texted each other while the games were played. Afterwards, we got together for drinks and dinner with the loser paying the tab.

Every week there is some type of game that gives me and my friends reasons to stay connected. However, to stay connected through sports, you must know their team and they must know yours. Let them know yours.

Lesson: Relationships are largely about connections. Sports gives us a great way to connect whether it is pro sports, college sports, high school sports, or youth. Find out who your friends cheer for and use phone, email, and text to stay connected. It's about more than the game.

93)Rip Currents

A rip current is a powerful, narrow lane of water along the shore that can pull swimmers out to sea. They kill over 100 people each year because swimmers try to fight against the current to swim straight back to shore. The lanes are narrow, and the swimmer can escape safely by swimming parallel to the shore instead of directly into the current.

We run into life's rip currents at work, with personal relationships, our health, and more. We can be overwhelmed or prideful which has us fighting against the forces challenging us, unable to see a simpler solution.

A friend of mine worked for a company for many years. For most of his career, he liked his job, did well, and worked with people he liked. The people changed and the company changed, which happens in every organization if you are there long enough. It was still a good company, but the changes didn't fit with my friend. He didn't like the changes and hated going to work. It put stress on him, his family, and the people he worked with. He is very loyal and not quick to change so he tried to fight through the circumstances, hoping for better. He tried one thing after another, and he couldn't make any progress. He is very talented with a lot of contacts. He couldn't see that the easy solution was to make a few phone calls and find a new job. When his stress level reached a tipping point, he moved on. He is happy, making more money, and living a life with far less stress.

When we find ourselves in life's rip currents, we need to step back and consider options we couldn't see because we were too busy fighting against the current.

Lesson: Don't fight against the current when there is a much better and simple solution available. And, if you are caught in an actual rip current, swim parallel to the shore!

94)The Golden Ticket

We all get invitations to weddings, showers, and other important gatherings. If you are trying to decide if you should go or not, you already know you should.

I've been to countless weddings and other events. There were times when I questioned whether I needed to attend. One of those times was when I received my first invitation to a destination wedding. I was concerned with the cost. I wouldn't know half the guests. It would use up a lot of my time. I debated it long enough to know that the right thing to do was to go. A wedding is one of the most important days in life. If I was important enough for them to invite me, it was important for me to show up.

When I arrived, I was treated as family by both sides. By the end of the weekend, I felt like family with both sides. I made new friends and strengthened my current relationships. While at the wedding, I thought to myself, "Thank goodness I made the right decision to attend."

There are many other events that I get invited to and if I hesitate on whether I should attend or not, I attend. Almost every event leaves me feeling happy that I attended and wondering why I could have given any thought to missing it. I've changed my thinking on invitations. I never look at them as obligations or burdens. I look at invitations as *Golden Tickets.*

Lesson: Treat every invitation as a *Golden Ticket*. Know that you have been invited because you are valued. You will be missed if you do not attend, so make every effort to attend.

A note about funerals. They are very difficult circumstances and there are obviously no invitations. Like other events, if you are trying to decide if you should go or not, you already know you should go.

A co-worker's parent passed away and the funeral was three hours away. The co-worker was important to me. We worked together for many years. I worked with his wife as well. I was trying to decide if I should attend. I didn't know his father. It was a tough drive from NJ through NYC to Connecticut. No one would expect me to attend so I wouldn't be missed. As I debated the decision in my head, my uncertainty made it clear to me that I needed to be there. I attended the funeral and, years later, the family continues to tell me how much it meant that I showed up. I thought to myself, "Thank goodness I made the right choice to attend."

Lesson: If you are trying to decide if you should go or not, you already know you should go.

95)The Dream Team

I know a lot of successful people and not one of them is a self-made success. They have had help and support from family, friends, business associates, advisors, consultants, and more. In their book, *The One Minute Millionaire*, Mark Hansen and Robert Allen write about the importance of assembling your personal dream team. These are people who you know that have knowledge, power, or connections which can help you stay on track and realize your dreams.

A friend of mine put this strategy to work. He worked for a company in the IT business. The company was bought, and he wanted to move on. He didn't want to get another job. He wanted to start his own company but didn't know what the business should be or how to get started.

My friend developed a list of people he knew who had a variety of different strengths. I was on the list. Some were corporate. Some were entrepreneurs. Others had technical, financial, or leadership skills. He rented a conference room, set it up with food and beer, included a large blank flip chart, and invited all to attend as his dream team.

We started by listing his strengths, interests, and resources. By the end of the day, my friend had a list of several company start-up ideas with a recommendation for one specifically, along with a general plan of action. He acted, started the business, added two other side businesses, and eventually sold all three successful companies.

I use this strategy myself. I have a group of friends, business associates, and mentors who I contact regularly for help and guidance. I work with each individually rather than in a group as my friend did. Their guidance has been valuable to me in my corporate, entrepreneurial, and personal life.

Lesson: If you have a dream, assemble your dream team. No one does it alone. And who would want to?

96)Am I Getting Ripped Off?

I know people who do not trust anyone and treat others at stores, restaurants, service shops, and work with a jaded attitude and disrespect. Yes, there are bad people in the world trying to cheat and do harm every day. Just turn on any news station at any time of the day and you will find it hard not to become jaded. While we should not go through life with the naïve view of a world without evil, we cannot go with a view that everyone is out to get us.

I was waiting my turn to speak with the mechanic at my local auto shop. I've taken my cars there for years and have always experienced friendly, honest, and fair priced service. The person in front of me was a new customer who had an attitude from the start that somehow the shop was going to rip him off. He wasn't going to let that happen. He was loud, rude, and visibly untrusting before the shop rep had a chance to talk. I'm sure he had been ripped off somewhere before. We all have been ripped off at one time or another. It's embarrassing and we feel we should have done more to prevent it. However, being ripped off in the past doesn't give us permission to treat everyone going forward as a crook.

Lesson: Don't let the evil in the world take away your peace. Treat people fairly and with courtesy until they give you a reason not to.

97)Overthinking

Sometimes, the obvious and simple solution is best.

I lived in a neighborhood where the nearby neighbors had kids the same age as mine. They played together in the front yards most days. One day, they were all yelling and being disruptive in very annoying ways. With so many people weighing in on how others should raise their kids, the simple solution didn't seem obvious to us. We were trying to reason with the toddlers, negotiating for better behavior, and trying to explain consequences. The news and social media outlets give us so much conflicting information about who we are, what we are, how to act, and more. We weren't sure what to do and nothing worked. It was as if they couldn't hear us, couldn't understand us, or just didn't care what we had to say. Another parent happened to walk outside to get the mail. Upon noticing the chaos, she simply yelled, "Knock it off!" The kids immediately stopped being disruptive and the rest of us laughed because of the obvious simplicity of it.

Lesson: Don't complicate things that are obviously simple.

98)The Interviewer

I've interviewed hundreds of people and It's hard to get to know someone after one meeting. I spoke with a successful business leader and asked how she determined if someone was the right fit. The same week I spoke with a successful entrepreneur and a consultant. I asked them the same question. I found it very coincidental and interesting that all three gave me the exact same answer. They told me that by the time a candidate gets to them, they know they have the education and technical qualifications because others have checked on those areas. They interview for character. They each felt the best way is to take them to lunch and watch how they treat the staff. Good leaders treat people at all stages with respect, compassion, understanding, and support. If they see rudeness, entitlement, and superiority, the candidate is out.

Lesson: Common courtesy should be common. Make it common in you.

99) There Goes My Hero

The Foo Fighter's song, "There Goes My Hero," reminds us that most heroes are ordinary people who, when put in extraordinary situations, step up to save the day. I hope you step up when the day comes. However, being a hero doesn't have to mean you are saving lives. I also see everyday heroes in a different way. I see them doing the small things every chance they get to help others.

A friend of mine from high school taught me to go beyond basic courtesy and help those around me. I've seen him help someone jump start their car. I've seen him pay for someone's subway pass in NYC when theirs wasn't working. I've seen him give an elderly woman a ride home from church when she missed the shuttle. Most of us do nice things for others from time to time when it fits our schedule and isn't too much out of our way. However, my friend does these things every day. They add up to hero.

Lesson: Don't ignore someone in distress. Be an ordinary hero every chance you get.

100) Your Priorities Will Keep You Straight

I work hard and have a very rewarding career. Some of my co-workers might be surprised to learn that my job ranks well below my family, friends, and fun. I try to keep this in mind as I approach my days. Sometimes, I can lose sight of what's most important and I need a reminder.

Early in my career, I was used to success and was thrown off track when a year didn't go as planned. My boss was in my office for the day to talk about the results. I was sick to my stomach when he went over the numbers. I wasn't used to this type of feedback. My boss was looking for ways to get things back on track, but I found it hard to think straight. Suddenly, the door burst open. My 5-year-old son ran in and gave me a big hug. My wife was right behind him, holding my daughter, to surprise me.

My mindset immediately changed. My family left and so did my stress. Once my priorities were back in line, I was able to take a very objective view of the business results and discuss ways to move forward with confidence. Better for me and better for the company. That was many years ago and I'm still with the same company and doing fine.

Lesson: If you are consciously aware of what's most important to you, you will be able to handle challenges in other areas of your life with greater ease and peace of mind. Your priorities will keep you straight.

101)Everyday Saints

I've read books about everyday saints. Love your neighbor with complete total selflessness seems to be a common theme. If you come across one in your life, count yourself lucky. I've been lucky to know one and it has made me realize a few things. First, like other traits I've tried to write about with these stories, being an everyday saint is about actions. Second, every action, from mundane to heroic, is out of love. Third, being an everyday saint and totally selfless may seem out of reach but it's something to aspire to in hope that a few of the actions will stick.

The saint I know woke me up every day for school, even though I argued. Made me breakfast every day, even though I never thanked her. She drove me to school, even though the bus stop was in front of our home. She sewed sweaters for me when we didn't have the money to buy them. She attended every one of my sporting events, no matter when or how far. She cried for me when I was hurting, but never cried for herself. She volunteered to drive kids with special needs for free, even though she could have found other work that would have paid. She raised me, my brothers, and my sister with equal and total love. She is devoted to my dad through the good and the bad. She lives her life with an abundance of love for her family and everyone she meets.

Lesson: If you are lucky enough to come across an everyday saint, let them know. I love you, Mom.

Final Words

You've made it this far, which means you are clearly someone who wants to continually improve and grow. That's one of the most critical keys to success. So, what are you going to do next? It's time to put these lessons into action. Consciously use several of them every day for the next year. That's 365 days of life transforming actions. You'll see change in how others respond and how you feel about yourself. Eventually, the actions will become a part of you.

Enjoy life's journey. I hope these lessons help along the way. If they do, please share your story with me. My email is JOE@JOEGALBOOKS.COM

One last thing, if you benefited from this book and you feel others might as well, then please give an Amazon Review to help them find this book. It only takes a minute or two.

Want More Books Like This from Joe Gallagher?

More books are in the works. I'd like to keep in contact with you through my e-Newsletters to make you aware of new releases and other resources. I hope you will join my e-newsletter list by subscribing. It's easy to subscribe from my Author's Website which is www.JOEGALBOOKS.com

Acknowledgments

Thanks to the editors and contributors, Chris, Sean, and Shannon Gallagher, and Don Finch.

Thanks to the original cover designer, Sean Gallagher.

Thanks to my family and friends for these stories.

COLLEGE of LIFE and SOCIAL SUCCESS

About the author

Joe Gallagher is a writer, storyteller, and speaker focused on actions that drive social and business success. He is a senior leader for a Fortune 500 company where he has coached and mentored countless marketing and sales executives, supervisors and managers, and fellow leaders. The foundation of his personal and business success lies in his ability to foster meaningful, trusted, and mutually productive bonds with family, friends, and business associates.

COLLEGE of LIFE and SOCIAL SUCCESS

References

Allan,R. and Hanson,M. (2002). *The One Minute Millionaire*. Three Rivers Press. ISBN:978-0-307-45-56-9

Atkins,R. Dean,S. While,B. "Watching You." *If You're Going Through Hell*. Ted Hewitt and Rodney Atkins. 2006. Album.

Artay,T. "The Dance." *Garth Brooks*. Allen Reynolds. 1990. Album.

Benthard,C. Hill,E. Criswell,M. "Just Fishin." *Proud to Be Here*. Michael Knox. 2011. Album.

Blac,A. "The Man." *Lift Your Spirit*. DJ Kahill, DontaeWinslow, Alex Finkin. 2014. Album.

Bokenkamp,J.(created by) (2013) *Blacklist*. Bokemkamp,J. Davis,J. Eisendrath,J. Fox,J. Carnahan,J. Spader,J.(Executive Producers). Davis Entertainment, Universal Television, Sony Pictures Television.(Production Companies)

Burton,T.(Director) (2003). *Big Fish*[Film]. Columbia Pictures, Jink/Cohen Company, The Zanuck Company.

Carlisle,B. "Butterfly Kisses." *Butterfly Kisses (Shades of Grace)*. 1997. Larry Day. Album.

Carnegie,D. (1936). *How To Win Friends and Influence People*. Simon & Shuster. ISBN:1-4391-6734-6

Ferrazzi,K. with Raz,T. *Never Eat Alone: And Other Secrets to Success, One Relationship at a Time.* Crown Publishing Group.

Grohl,D. Mendel,N. Smear,P. "My Hero." *The Colour and the Shape.* Gill Norton. 1997. Album.

Heller,B. (Created by) (2014) *Gotham.* Cannon,D. Heller,B. Stephens,J. Edlund,B. Woodruff,K. (Executive Producers). Primrose Hill, DC Entertainment, Warner Bros. (Production Companies).

Keshner,I. (Director) (1980). *Star Wars Episode V:The Empire Strikes Back*[Film]. Lucasfilm Ltd.

Mangold,J. (Director) (2010). *Knight and Day*[Film]. Regency Enterprises, Dune Entertainment, New Regency, Pink Machine, Todd Gardner Productions, Treeline Film.

McKensie,R. with Kubey,C. (2001). *7 Steps to a Pain-Free Life.* The Penguin Group. ISBN:0-525-94560-1

Philips,B. (1999). *Body For Life:12 Weeks to Mental and Physical Strength.* Harper Collins. ISBN:0-06-01939339-5

Wachowskis,The. (Directors) (1999). *The Matrix*[Film].Warner Brothers, Village Roadshow Pictures, Groucho II Film Partnership, Silver Pictures.

JOE GALLAGHER

Made in the USA
Las Vegas, NV
01 October 2023

78403318R00096